Cute and Whimsical Kids

By

Kim Jordan Blair

I want to give a special thank you to Wanda Fridley, for granting me permission to use her colored version of my happy baby on the cover of this book.

I also want to thank Kat Suydam for her constant encouragement. Ever since she saw my first picture she encouraged me to make a coloring book. So I did and now here is my third coloring book. Something I never would have done without her encouragement.

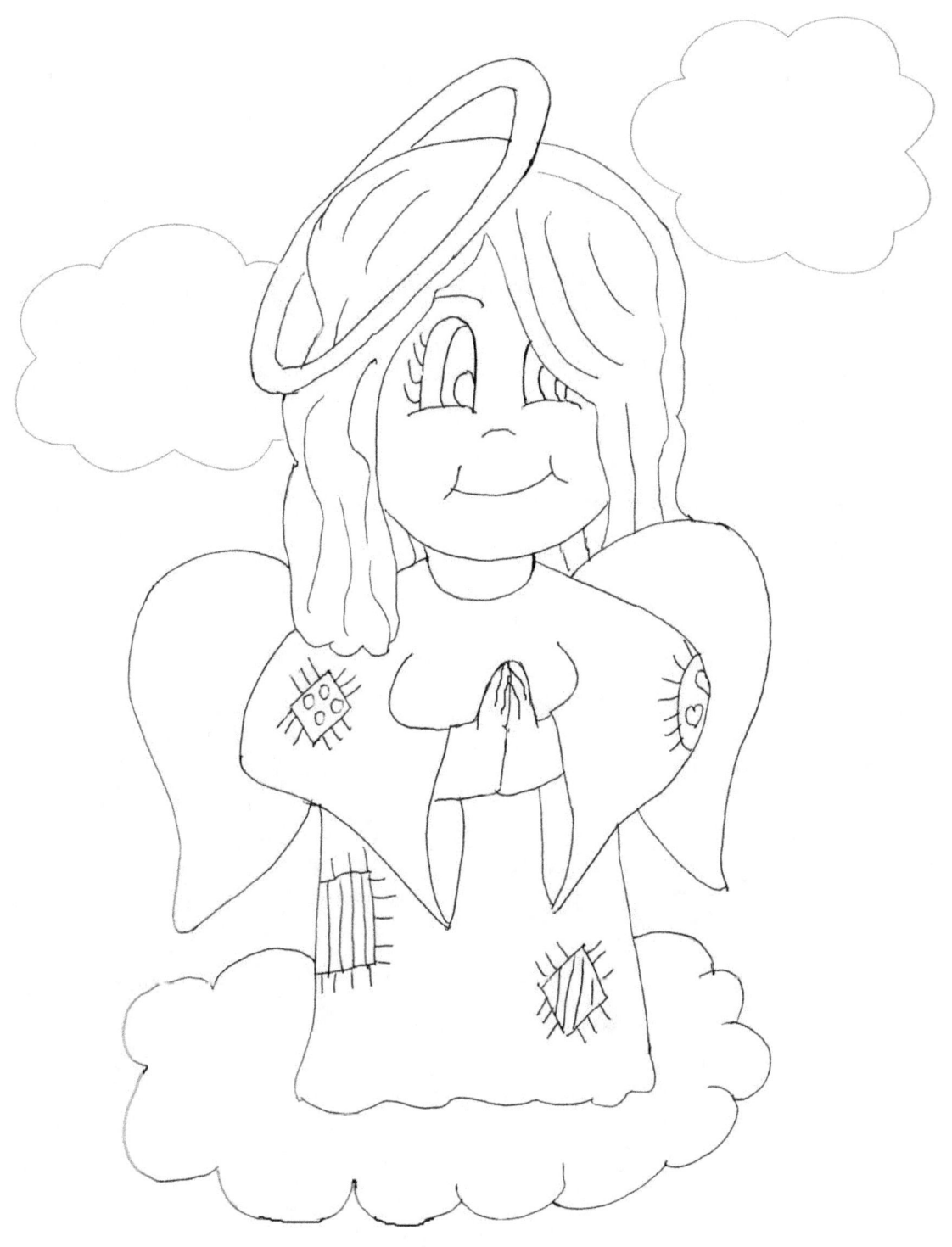

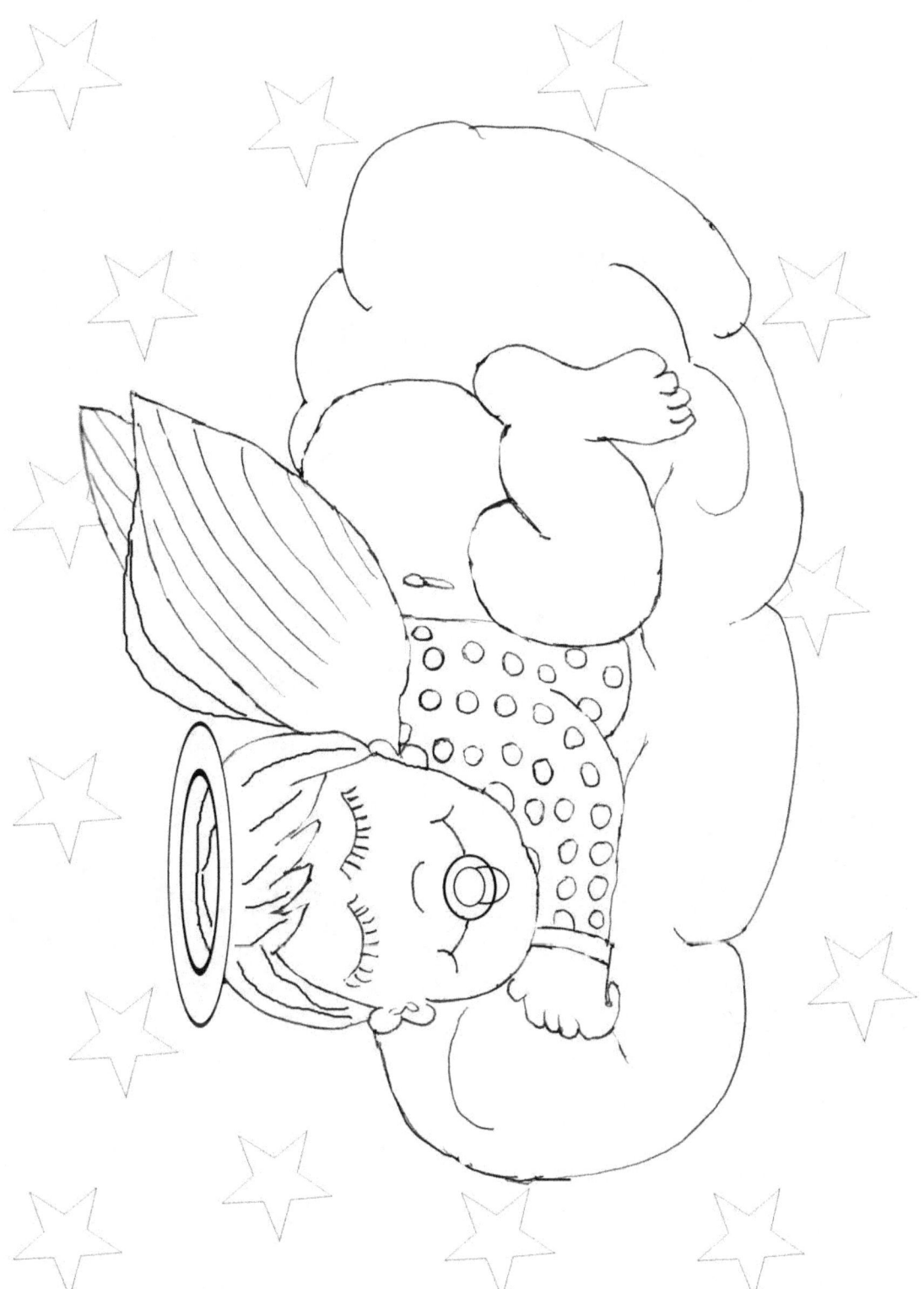

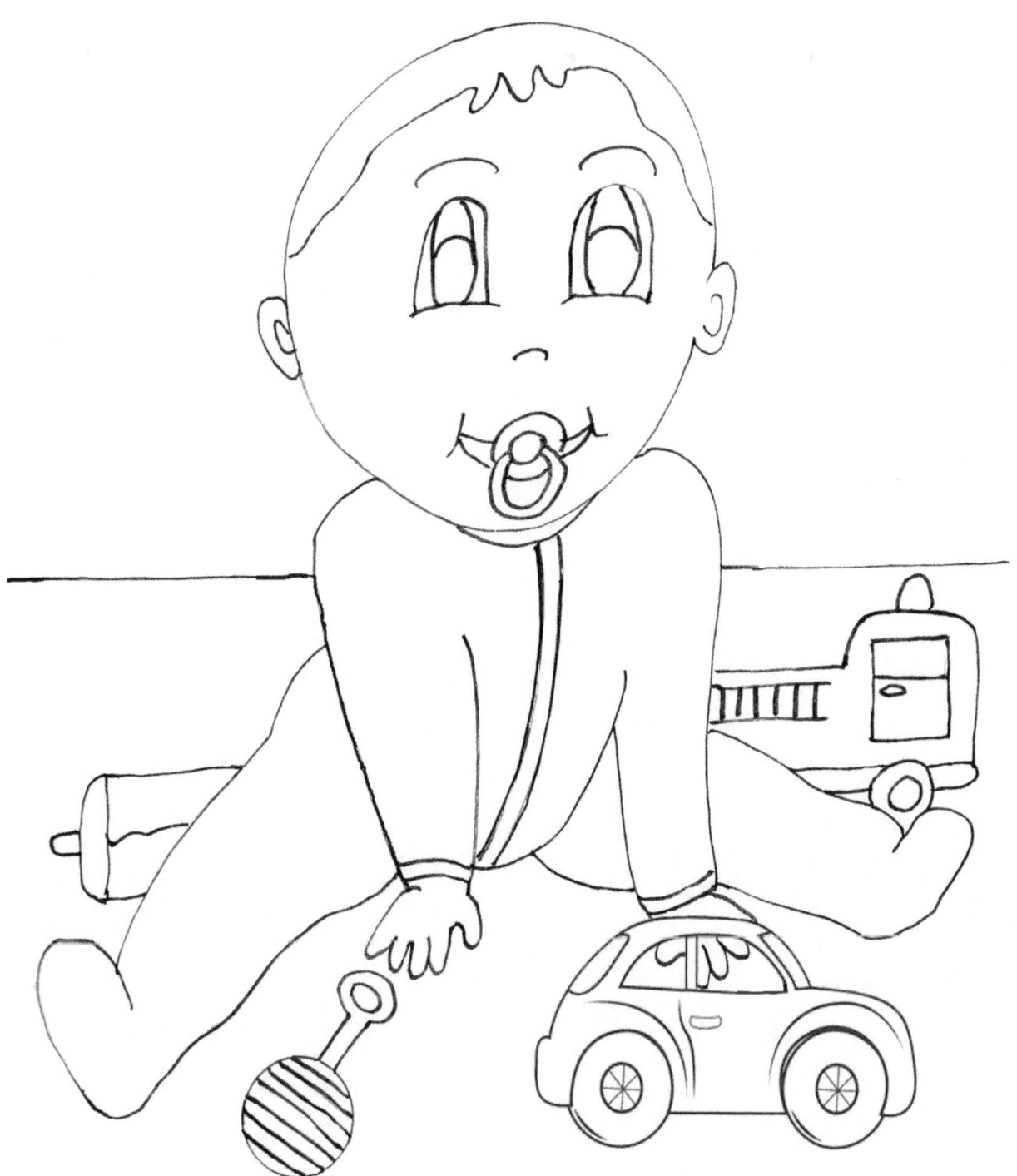

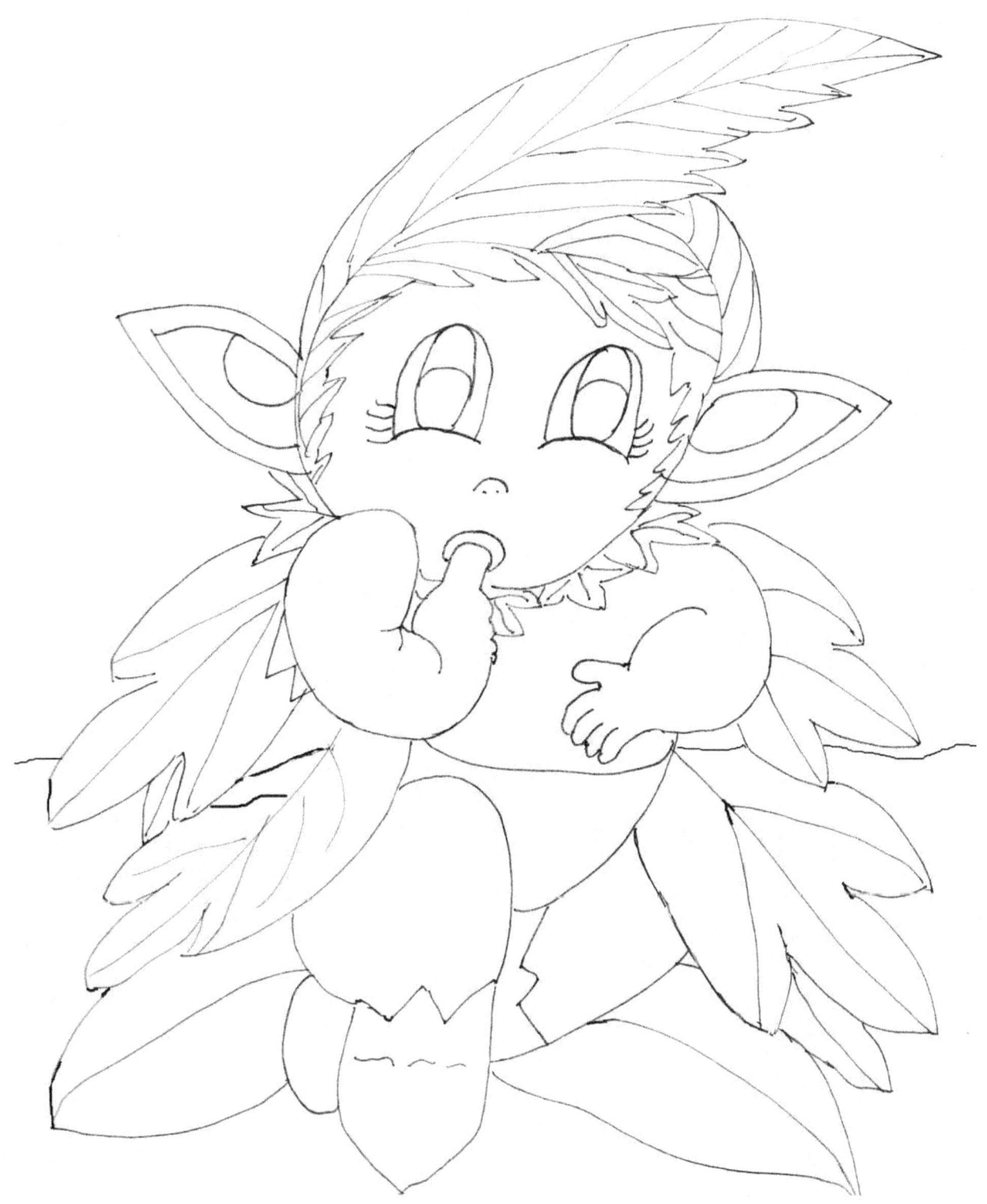

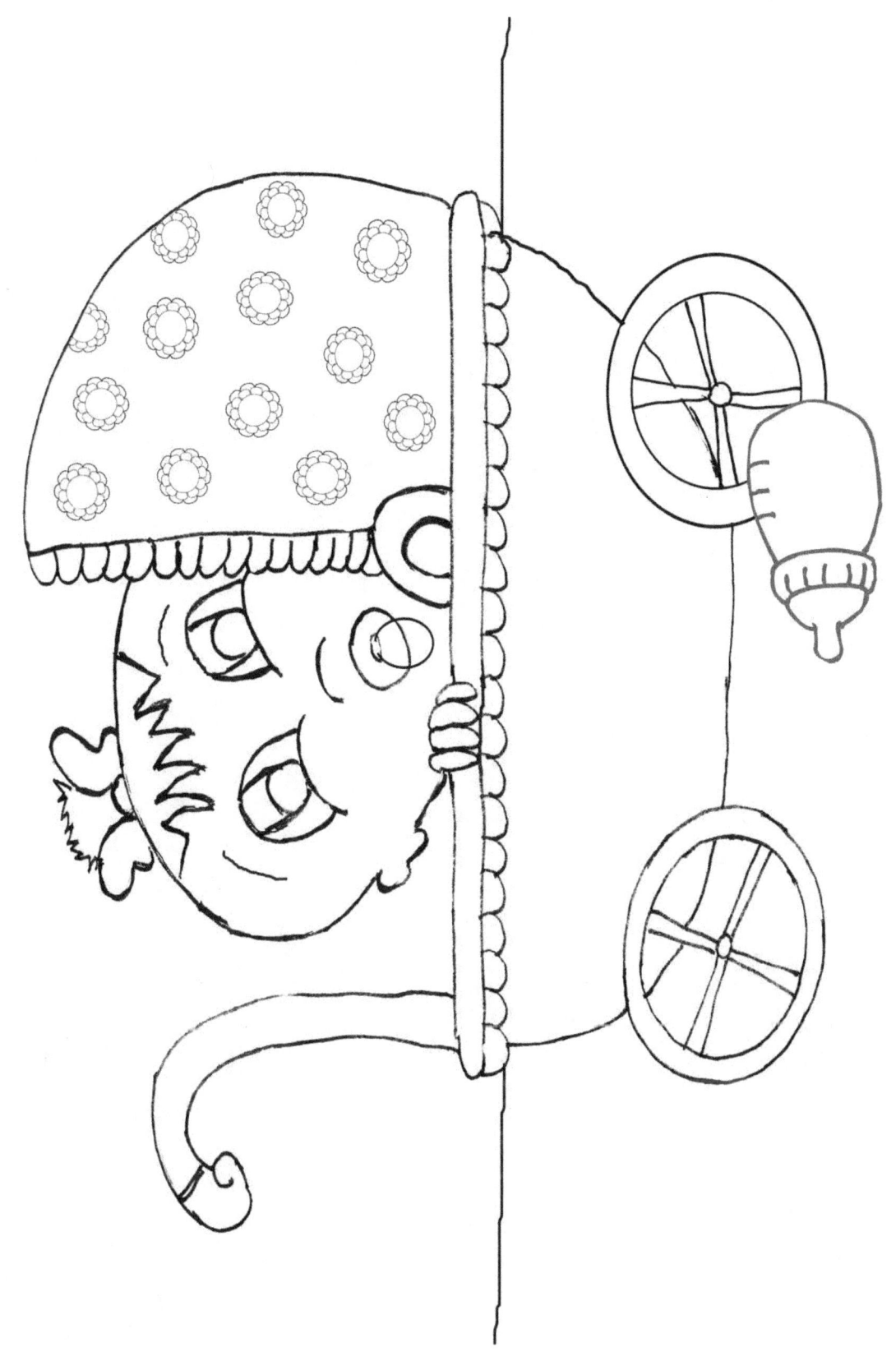

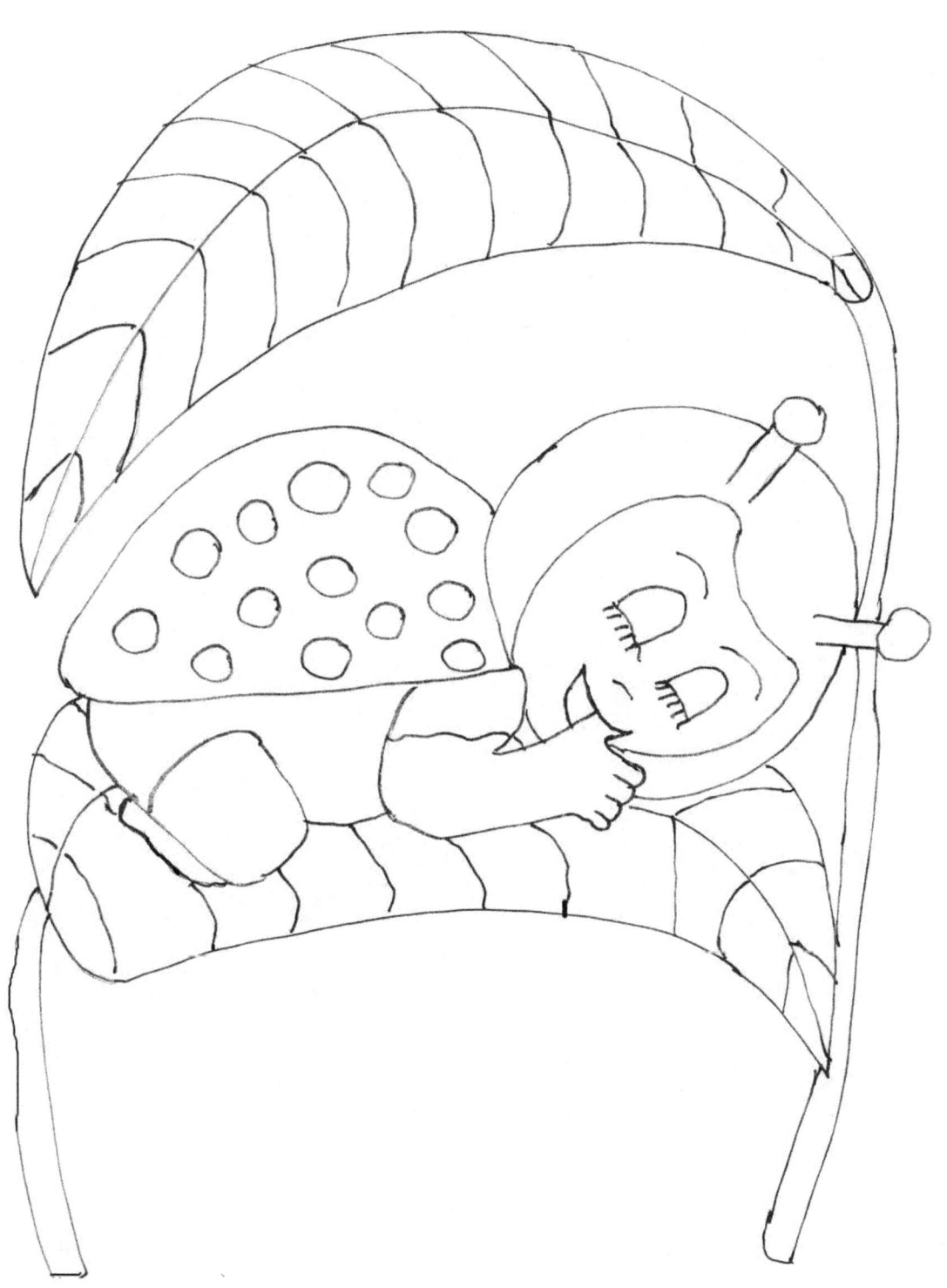

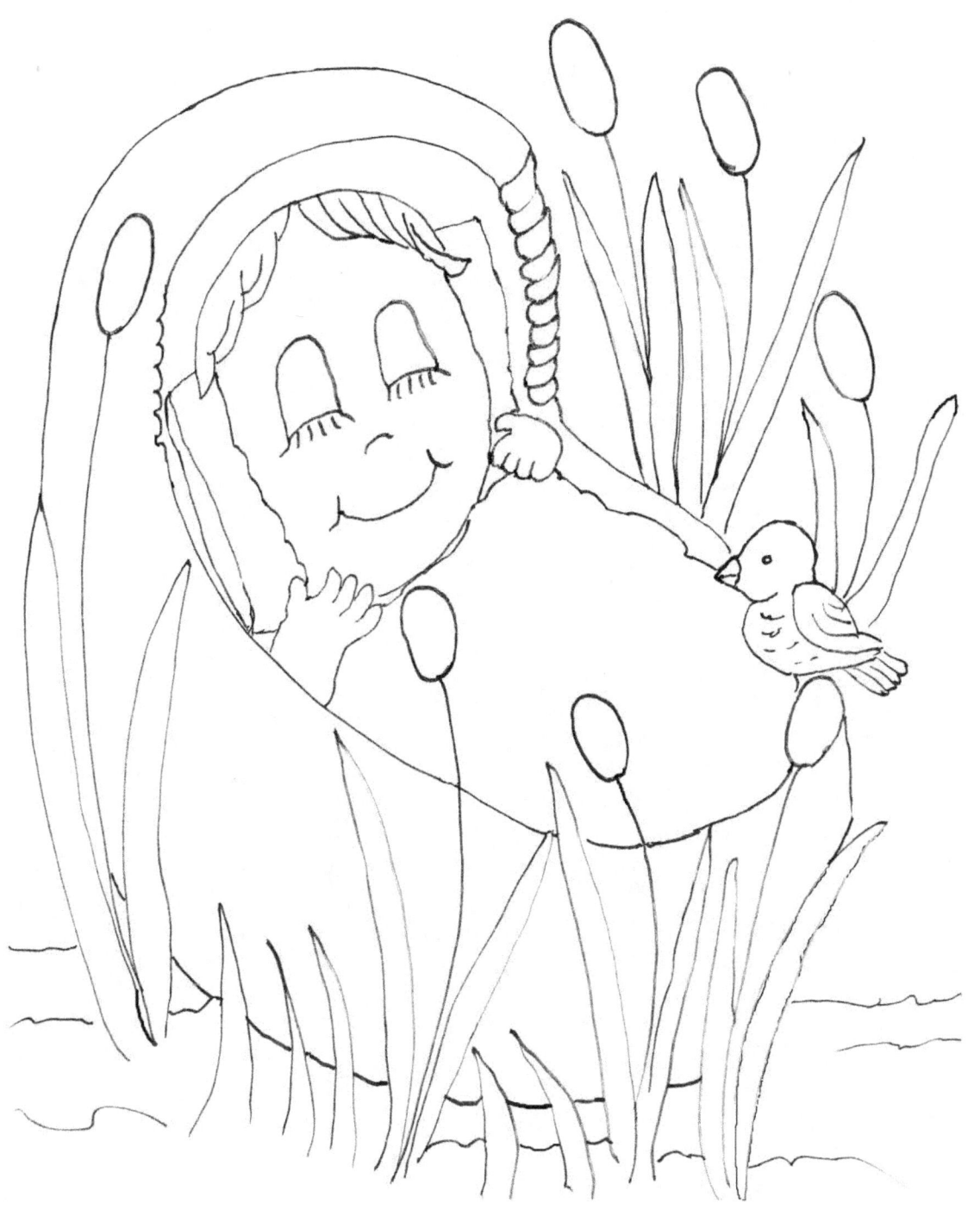

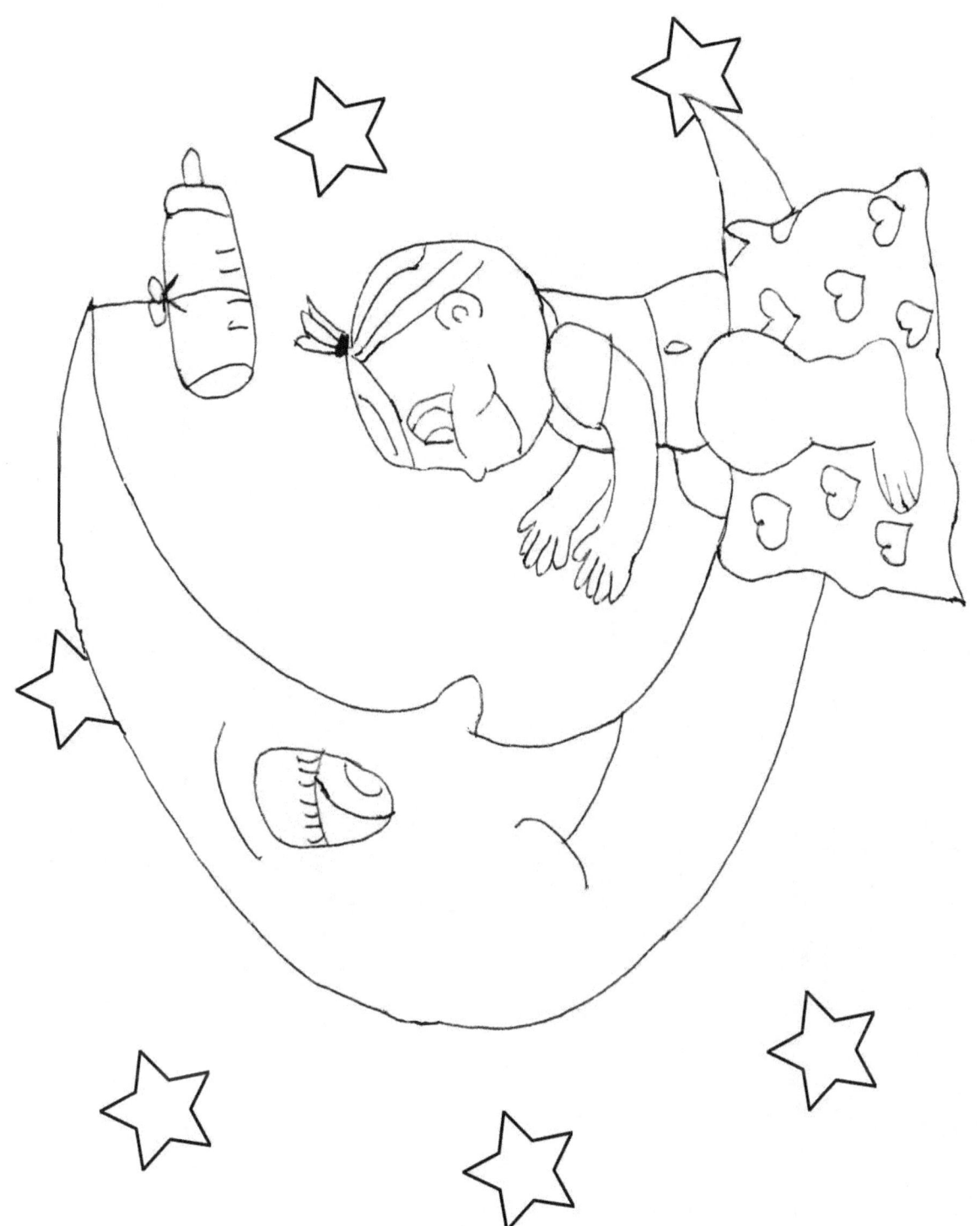

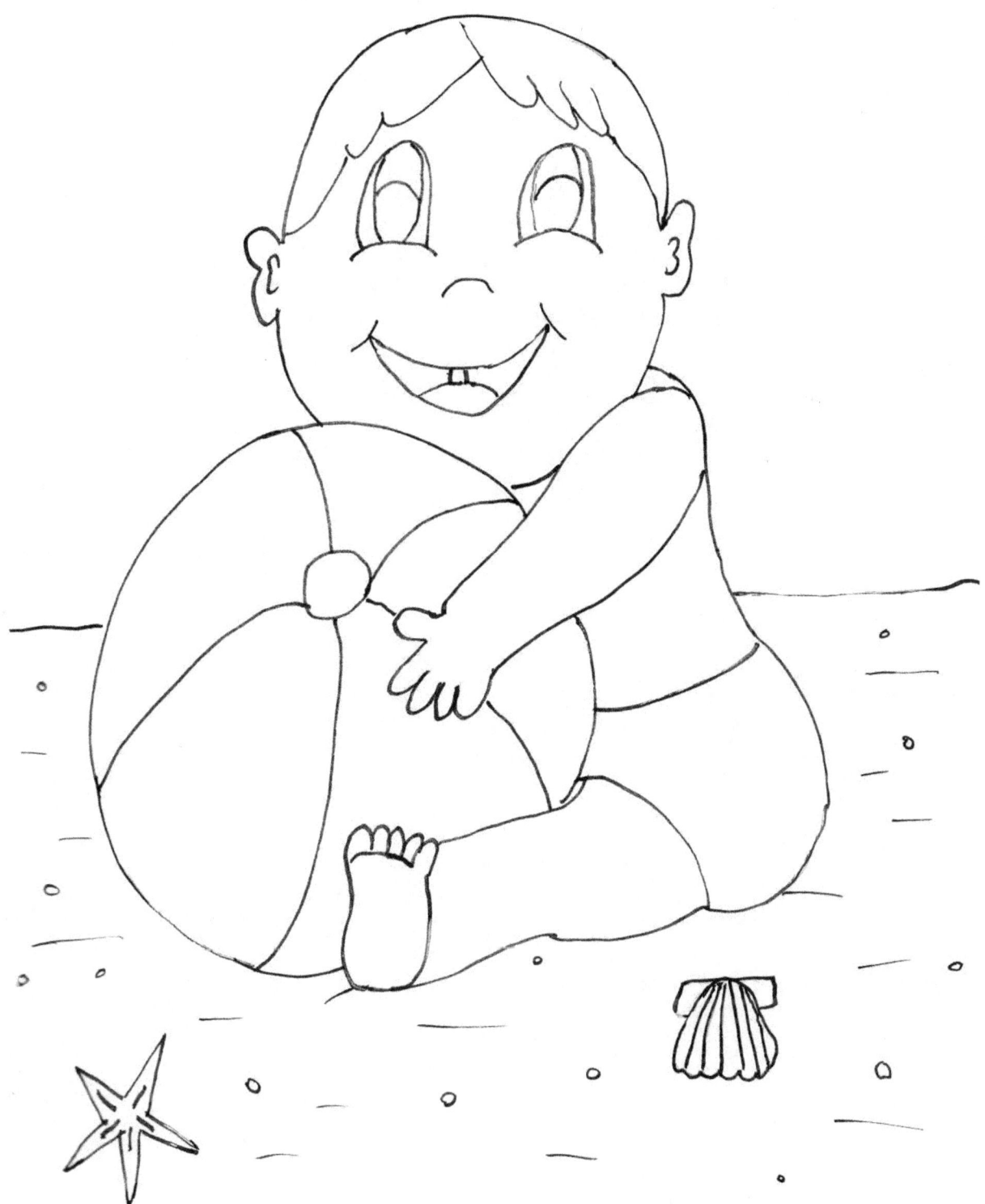

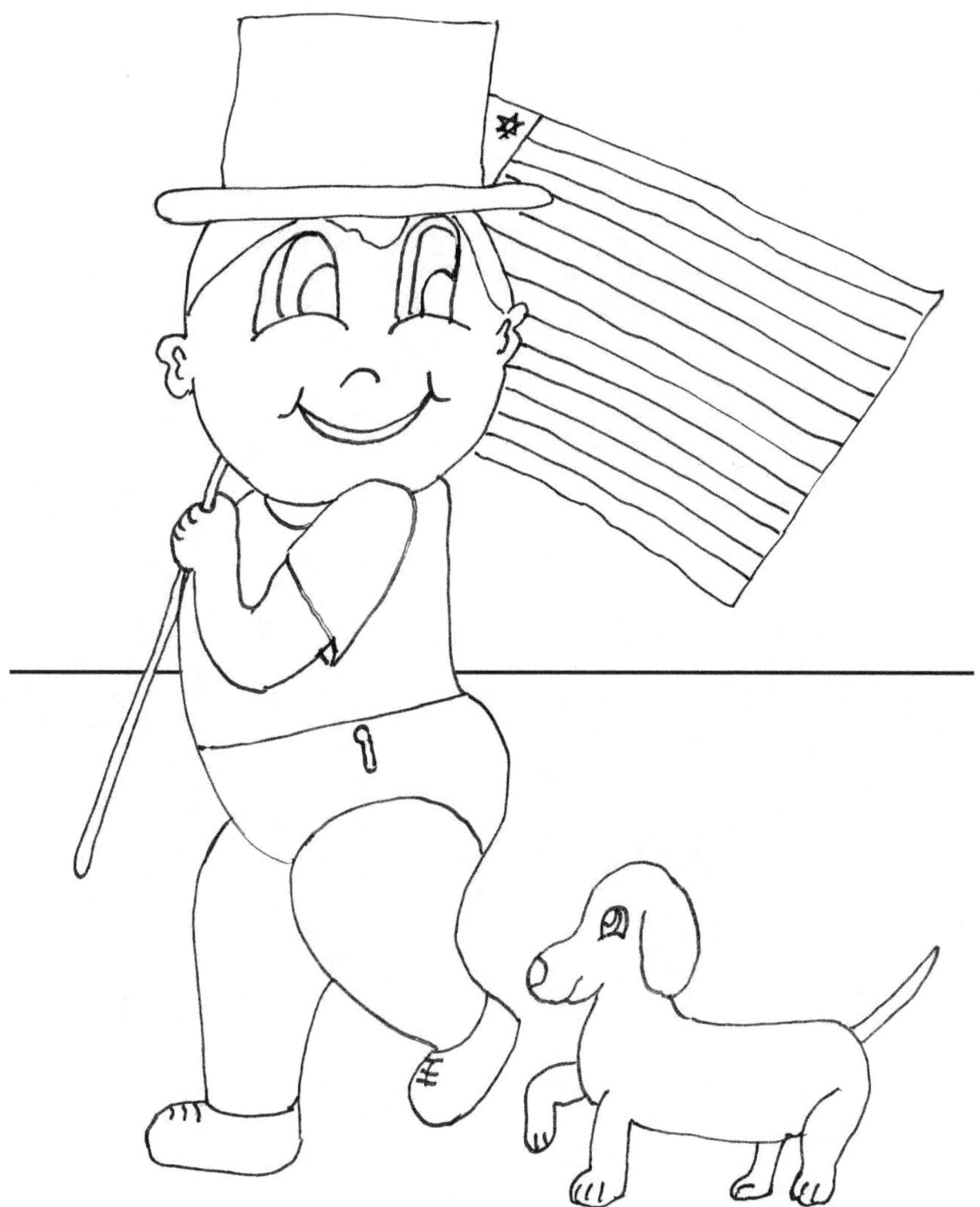

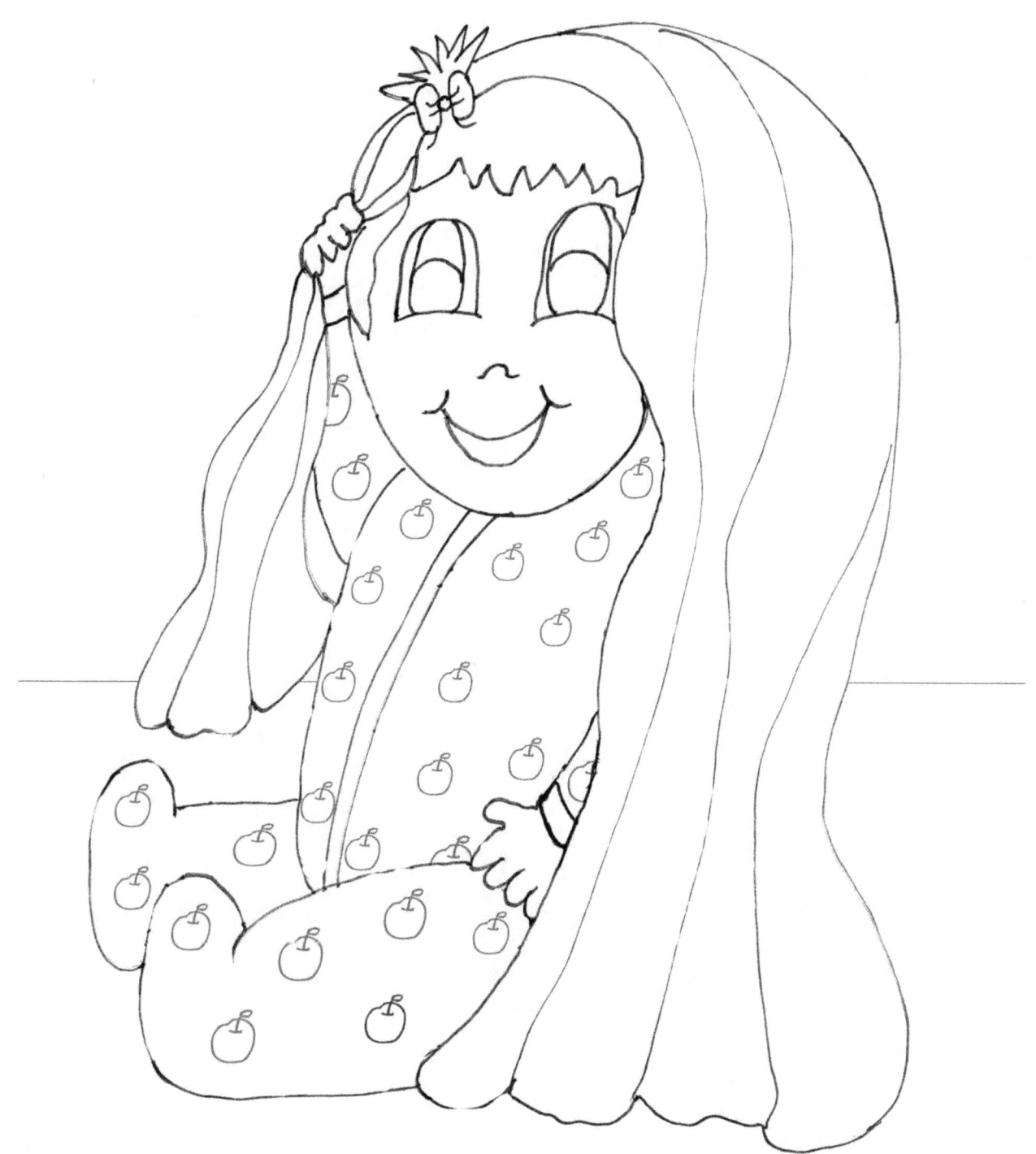

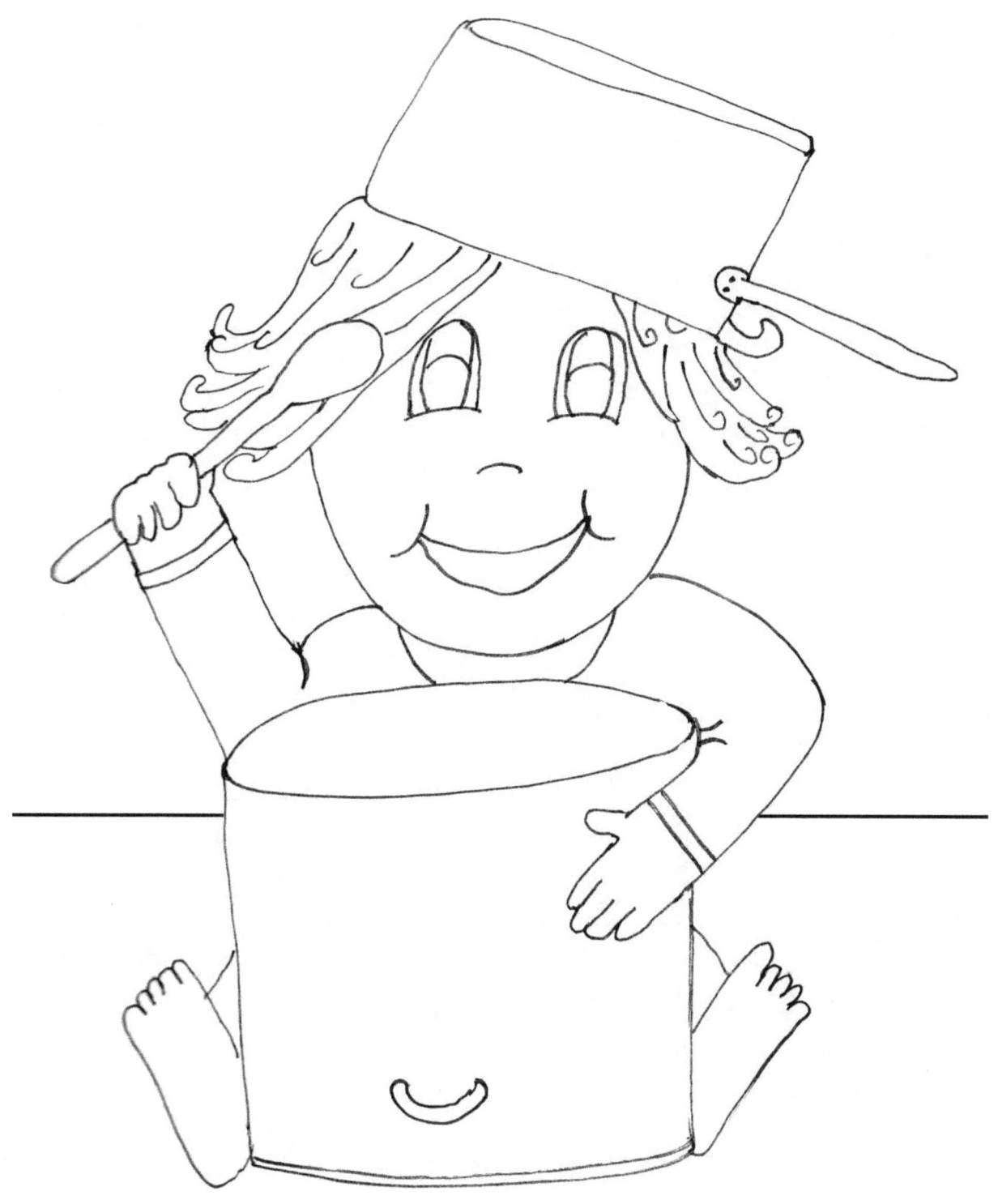

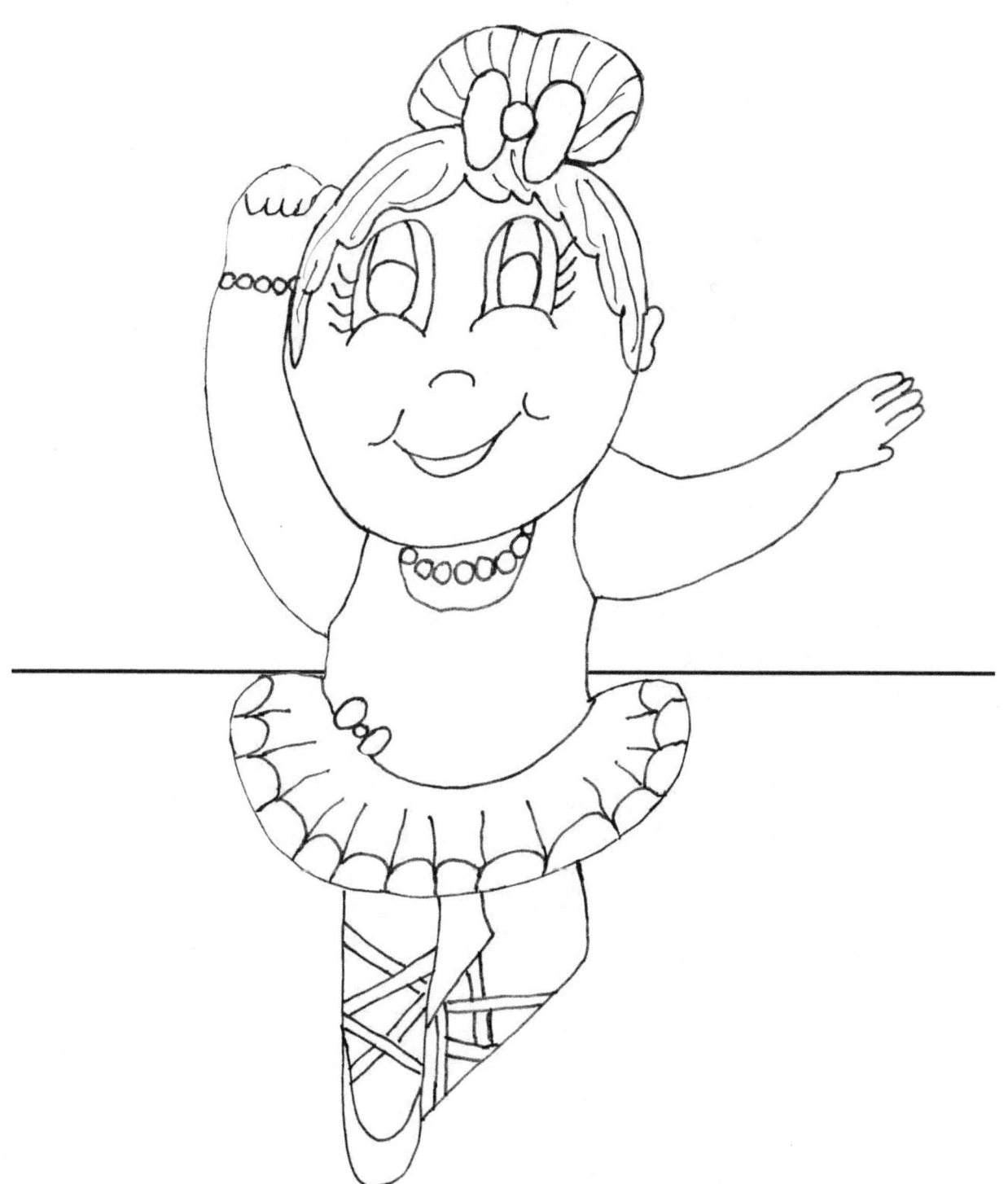

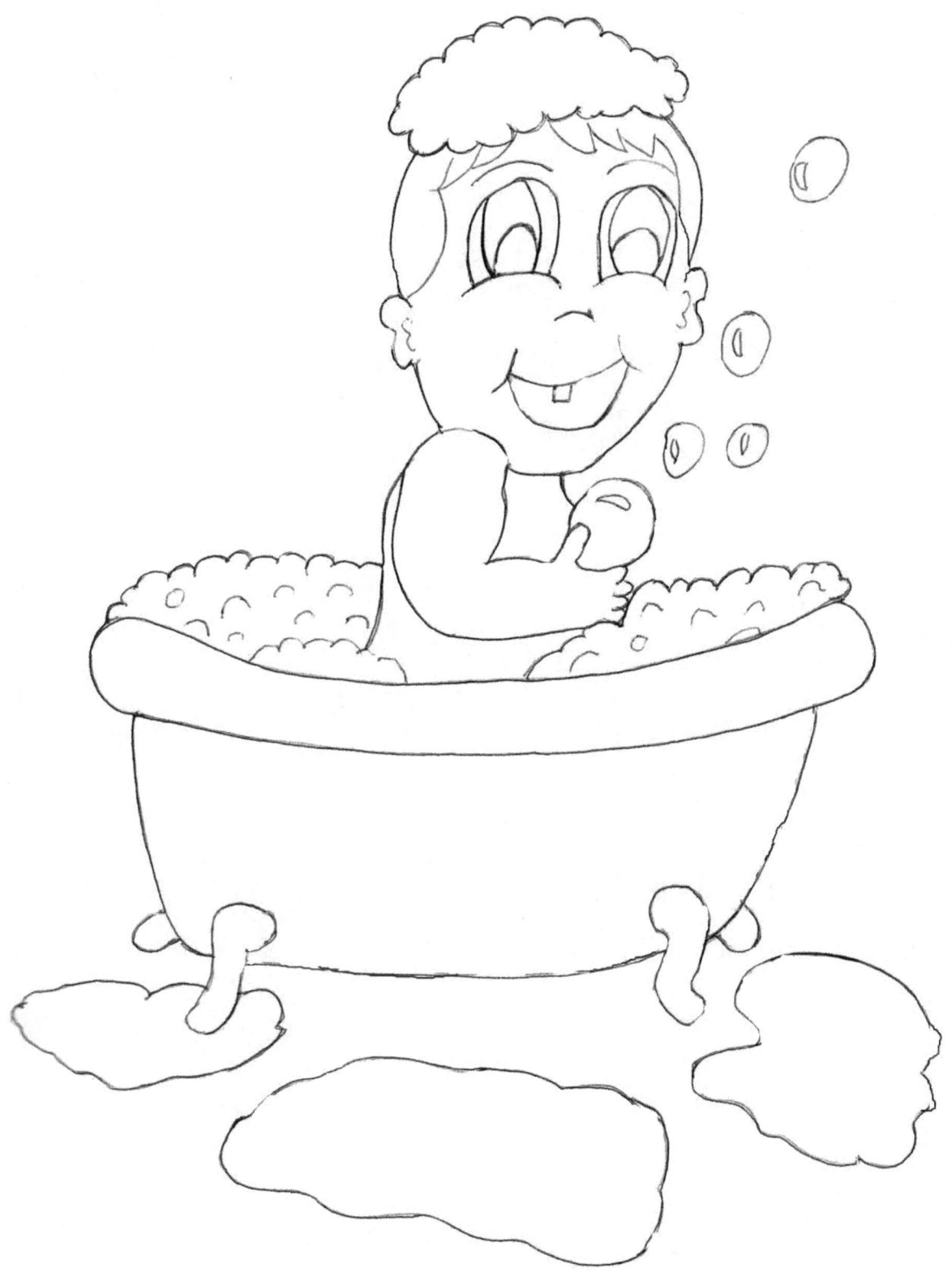

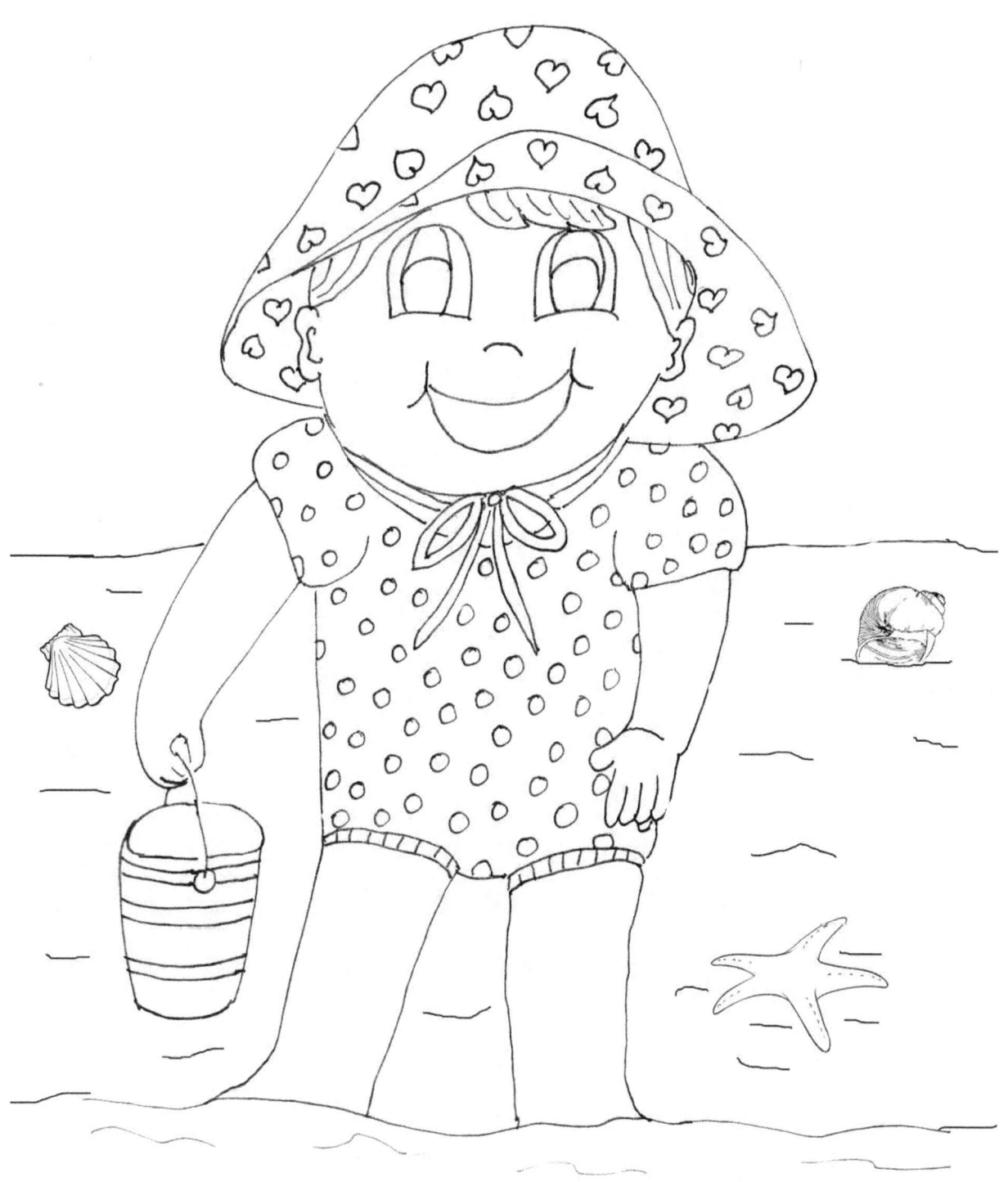

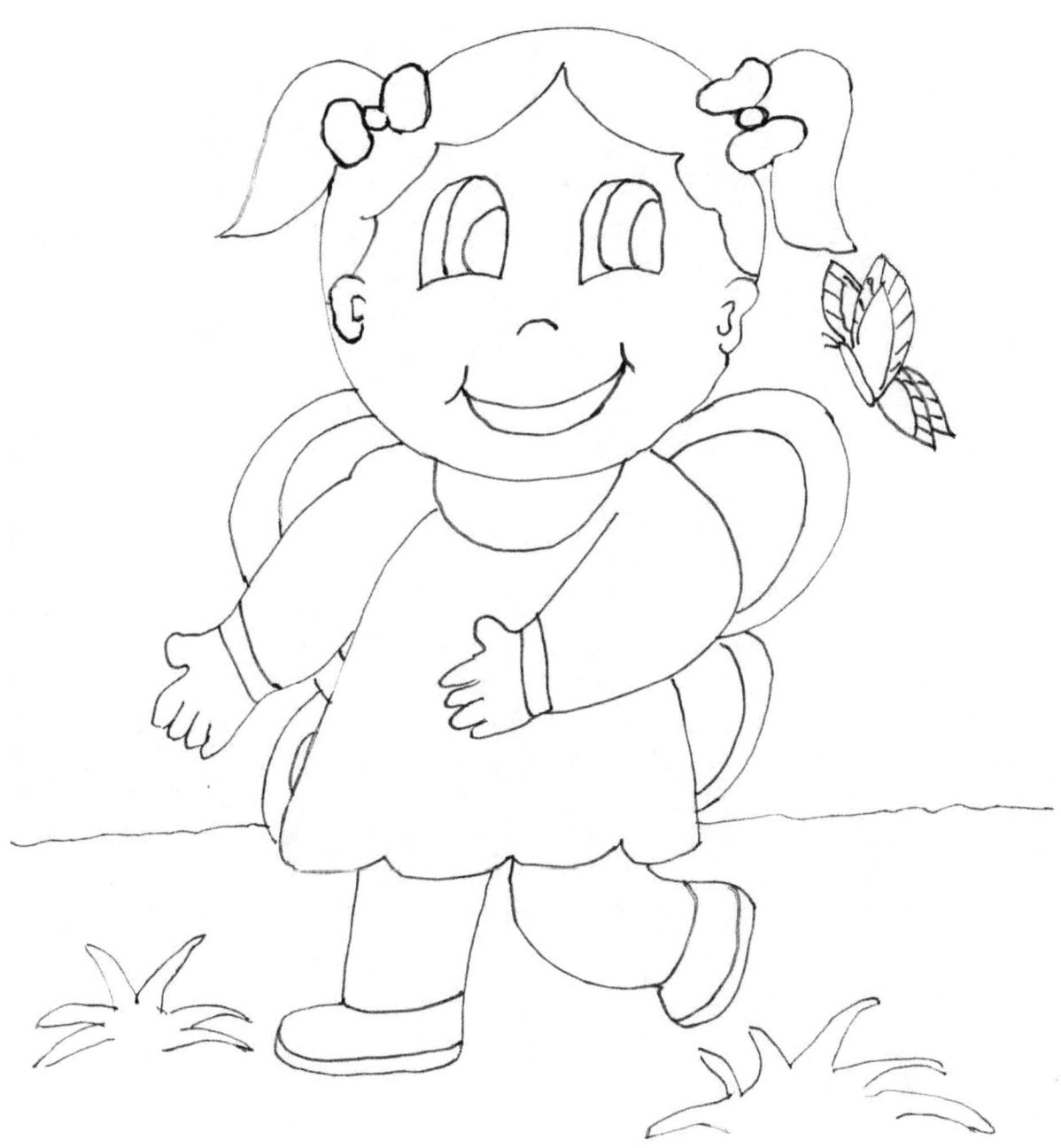

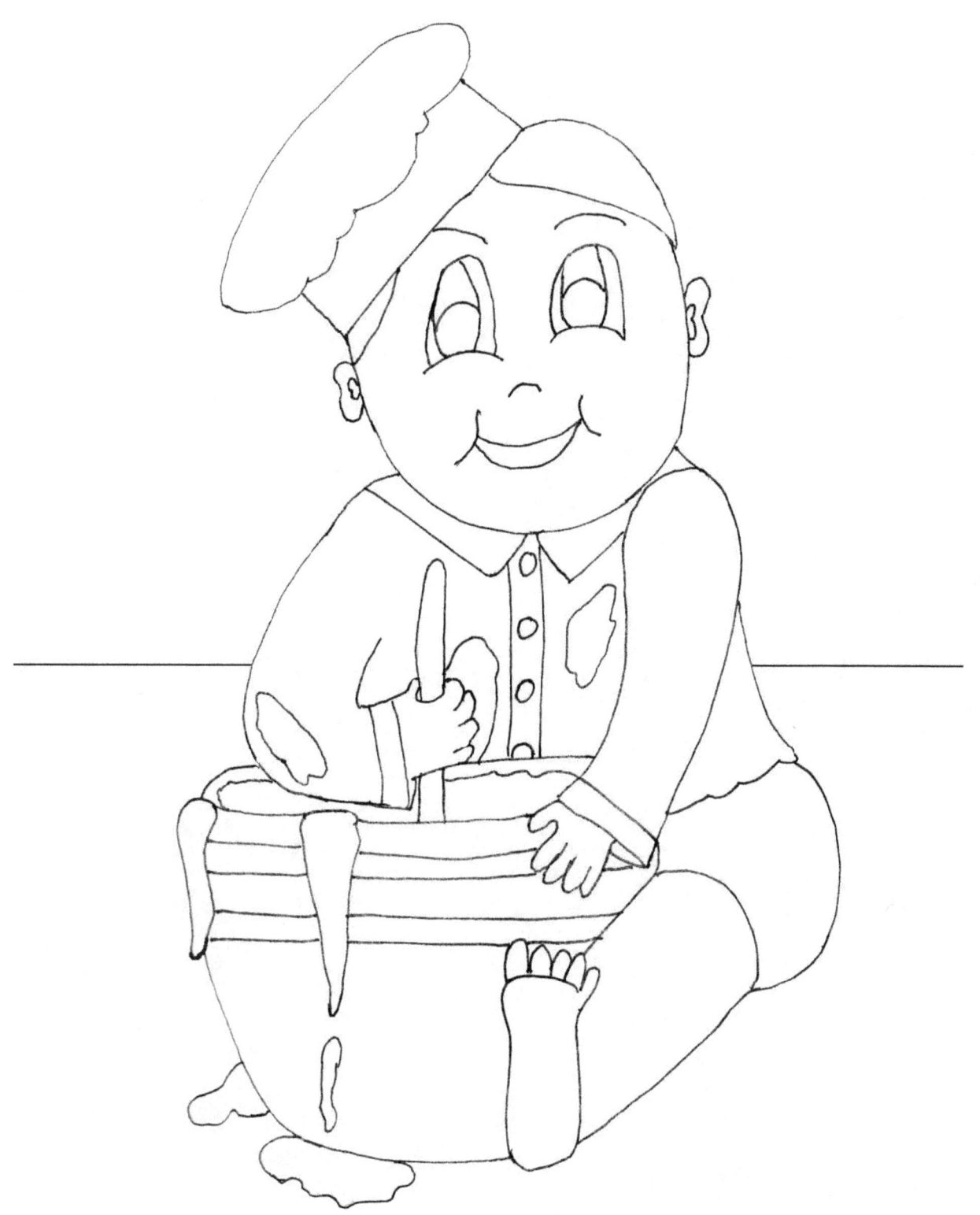

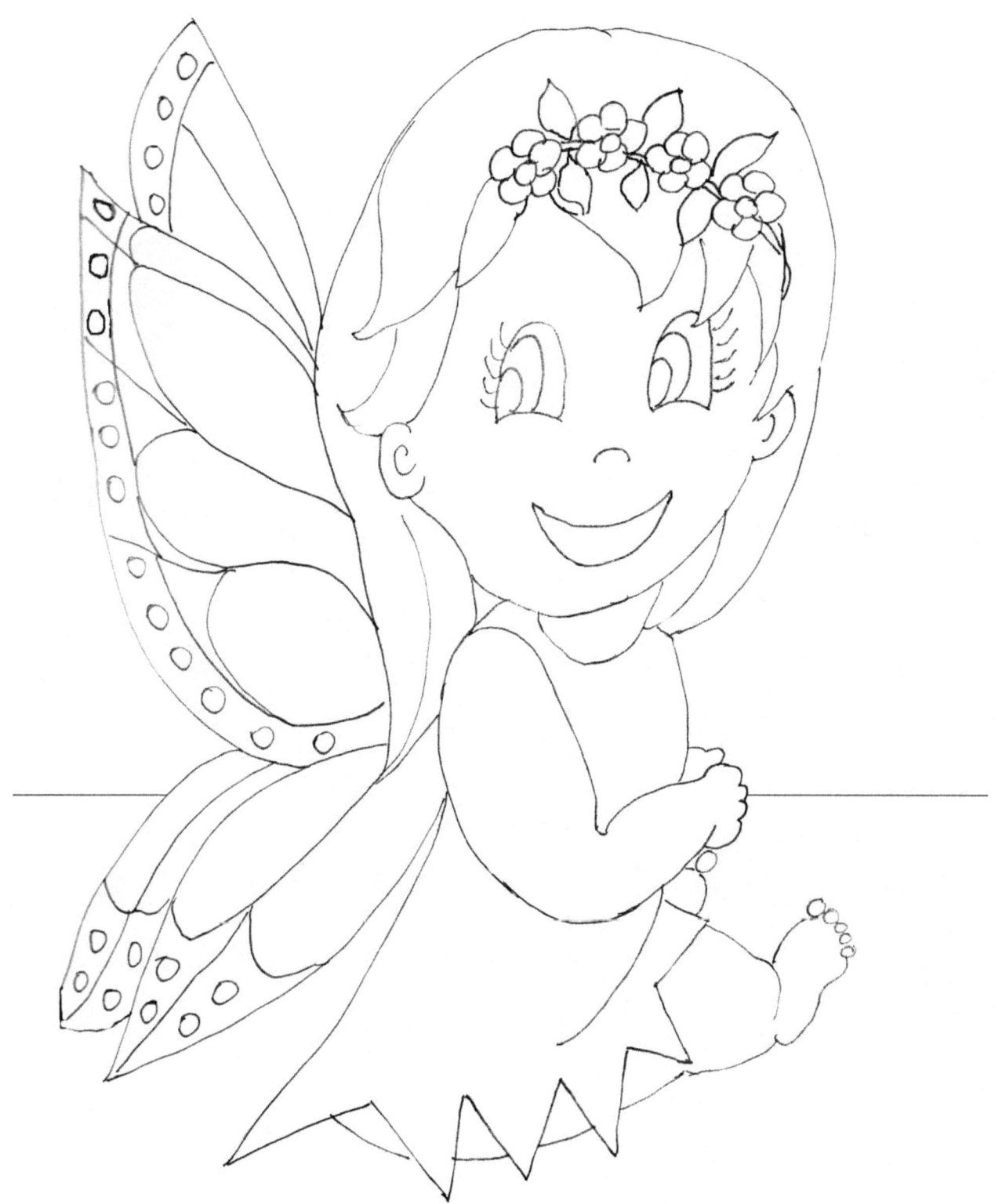

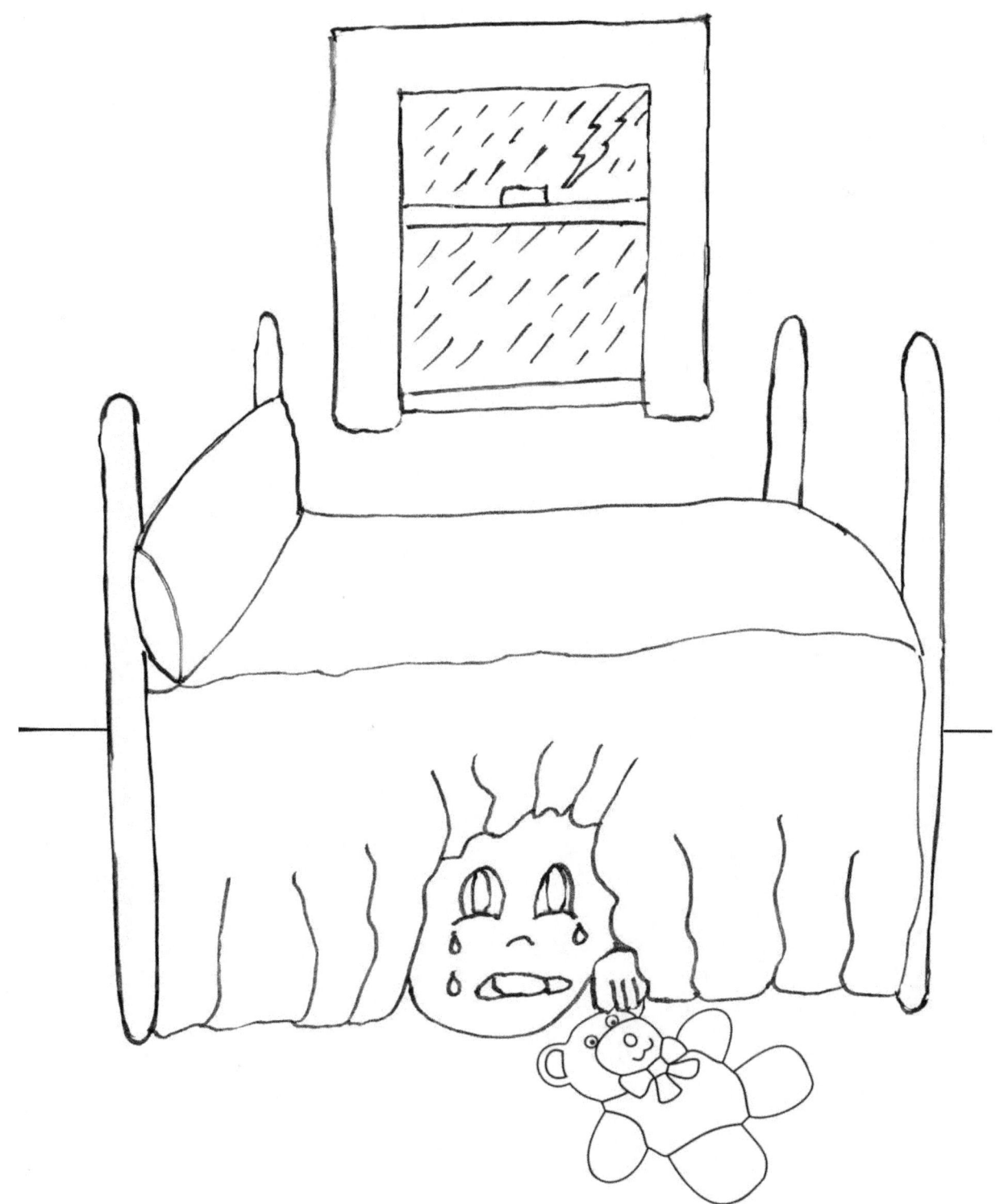

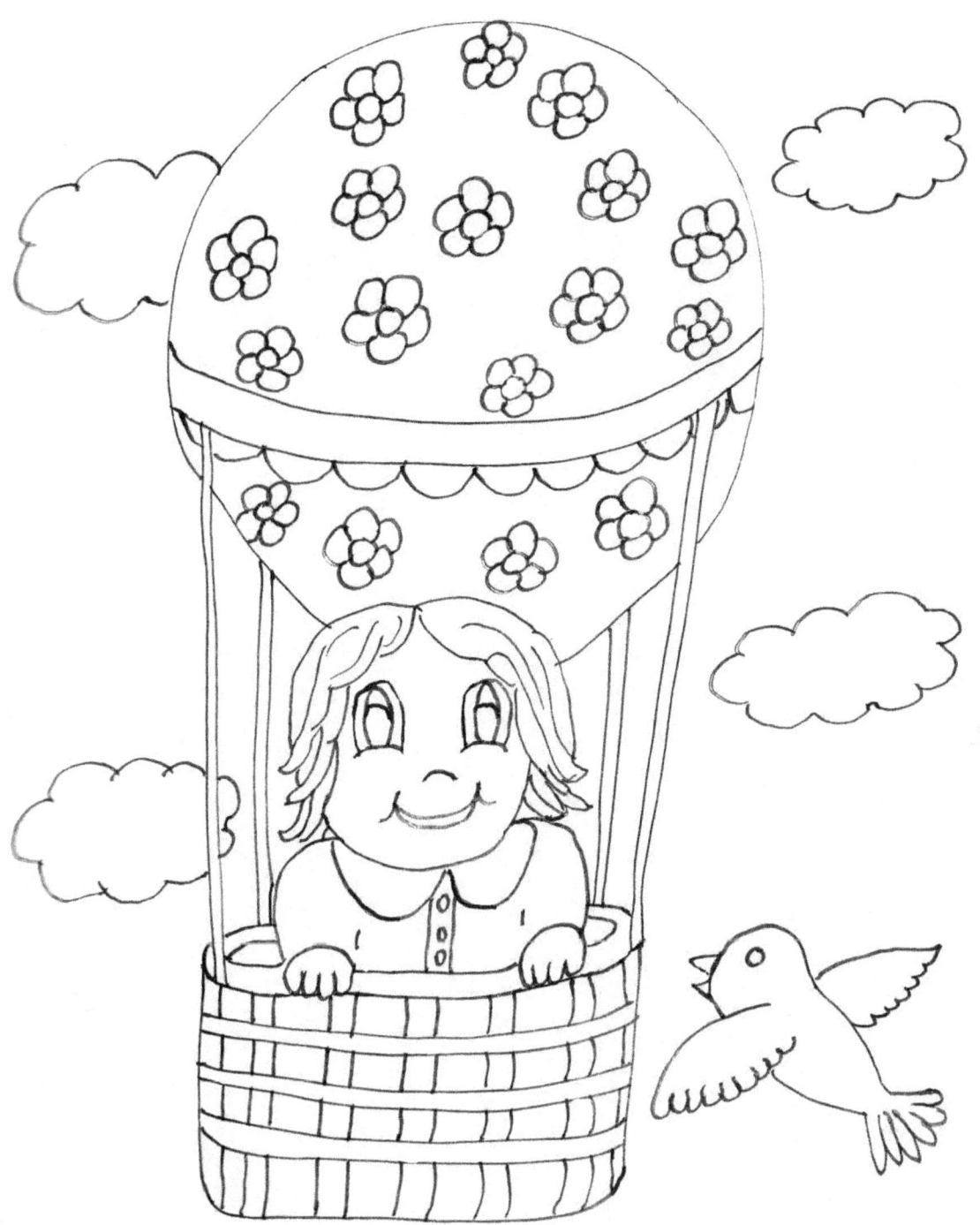

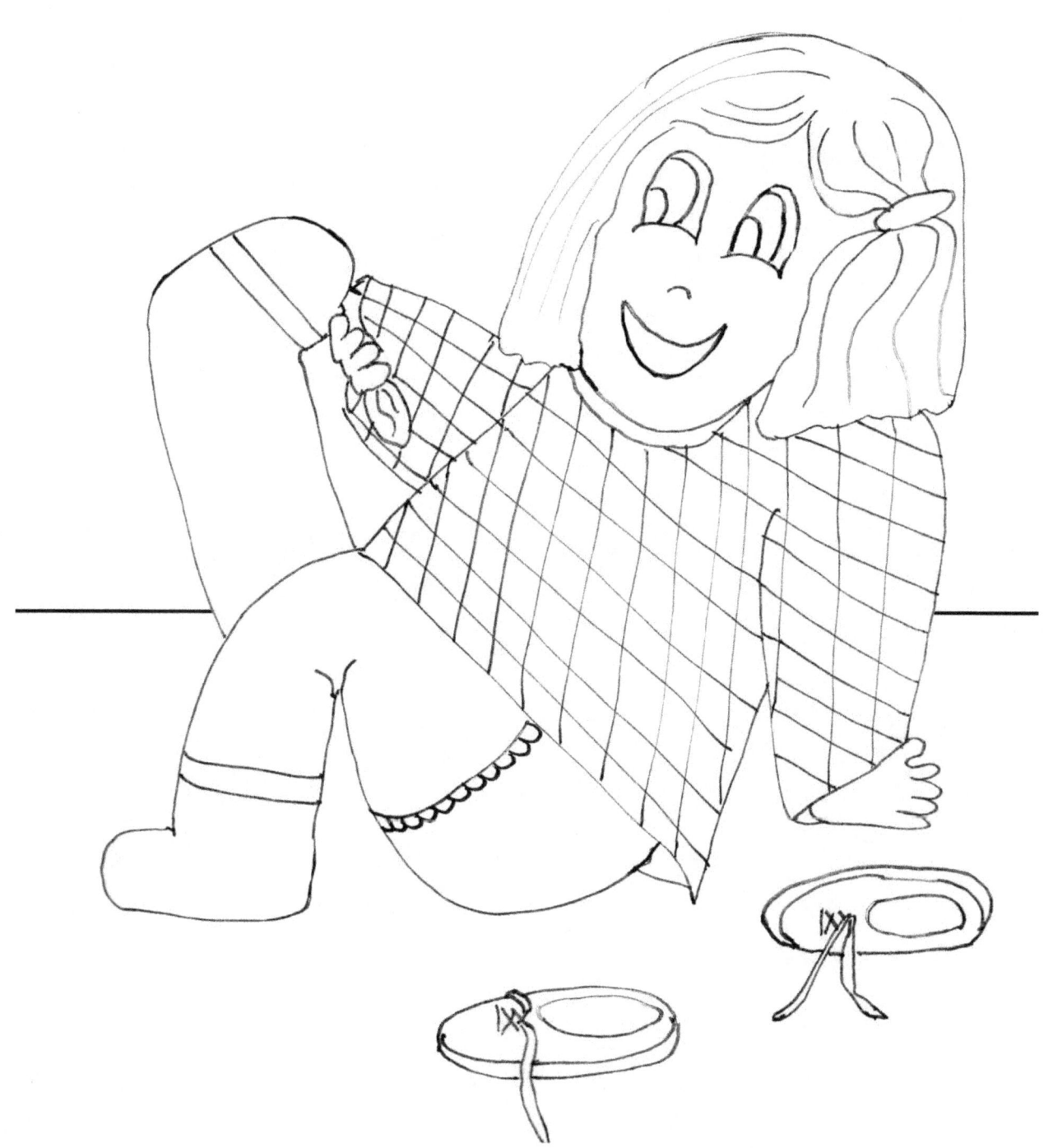

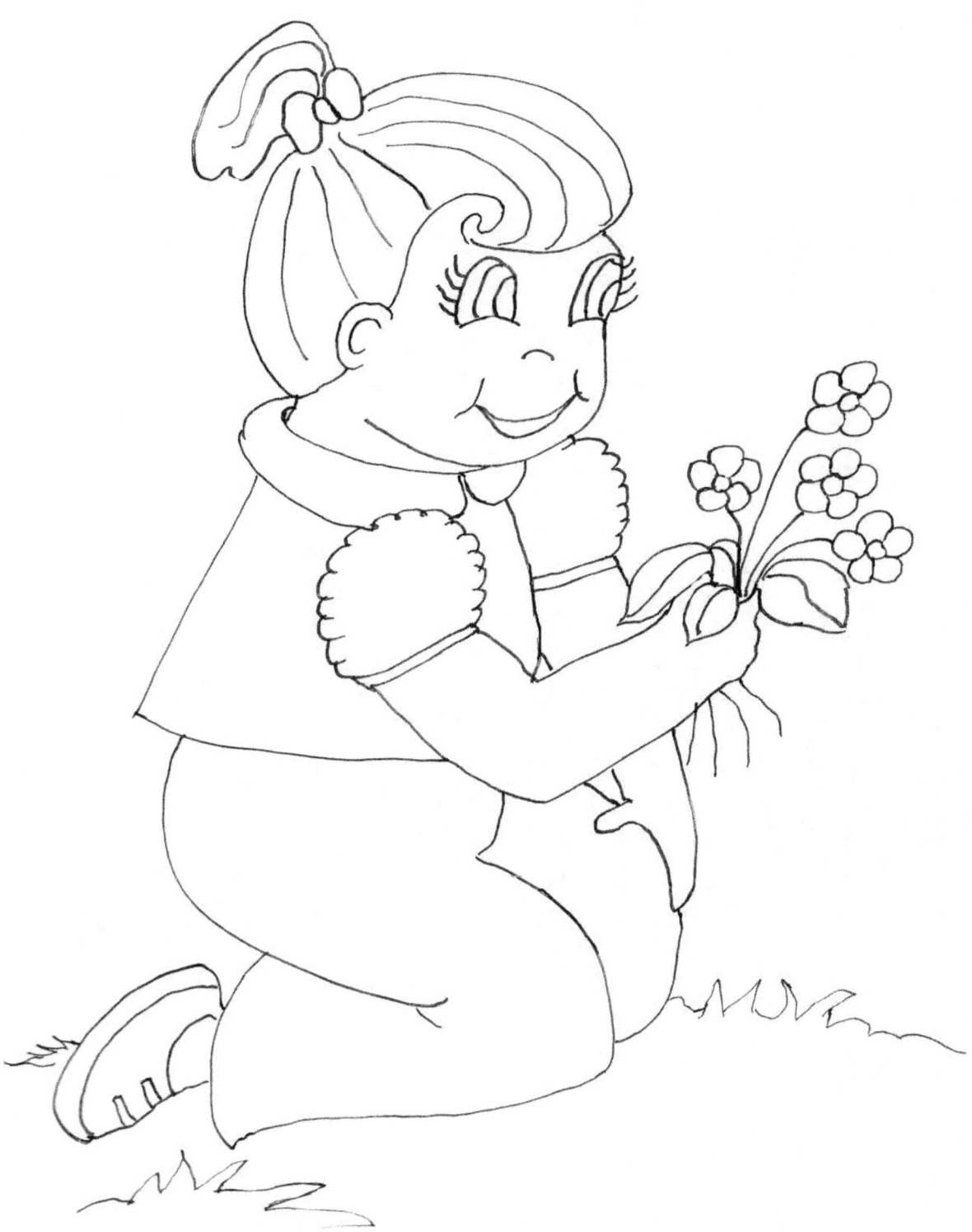

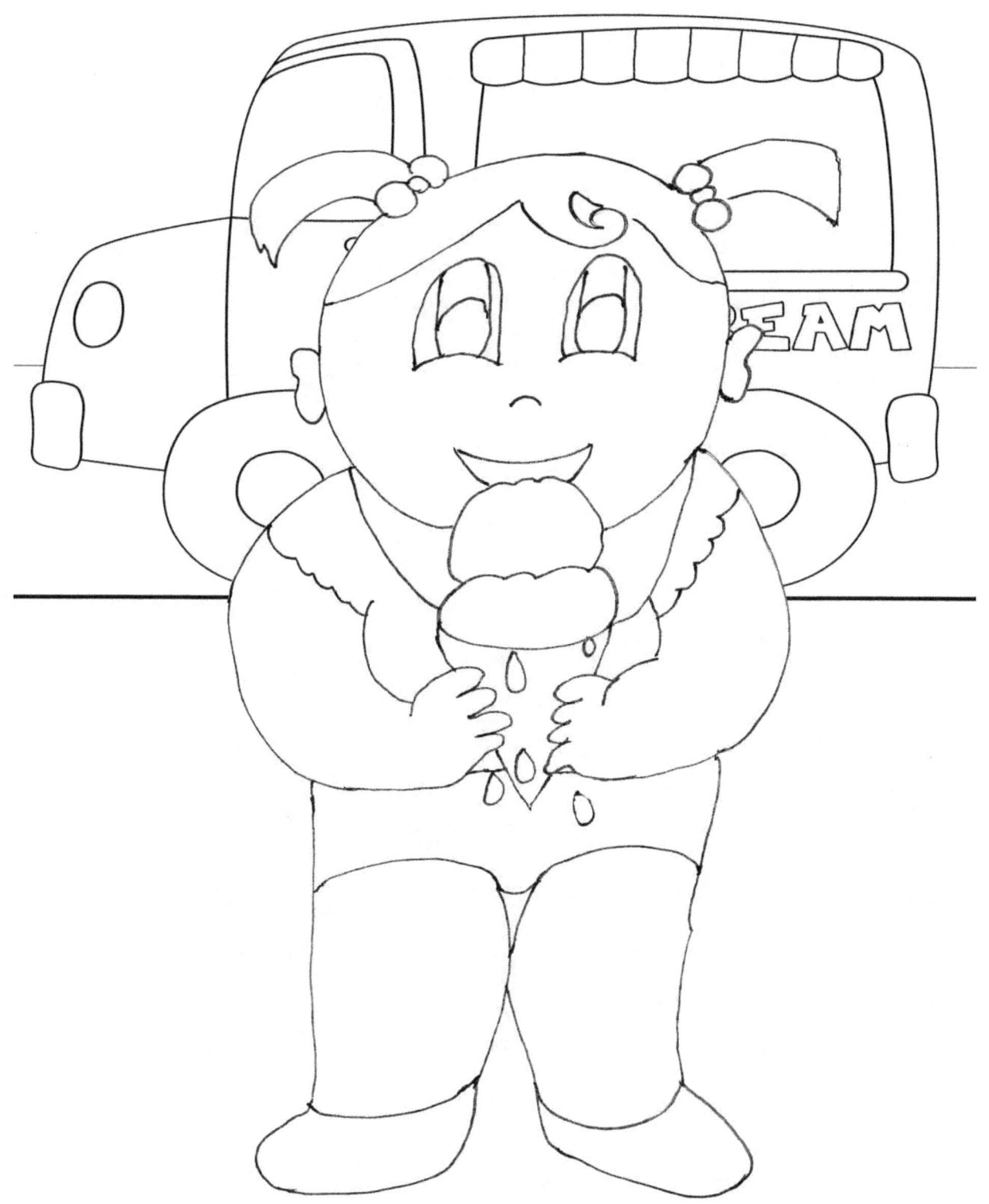

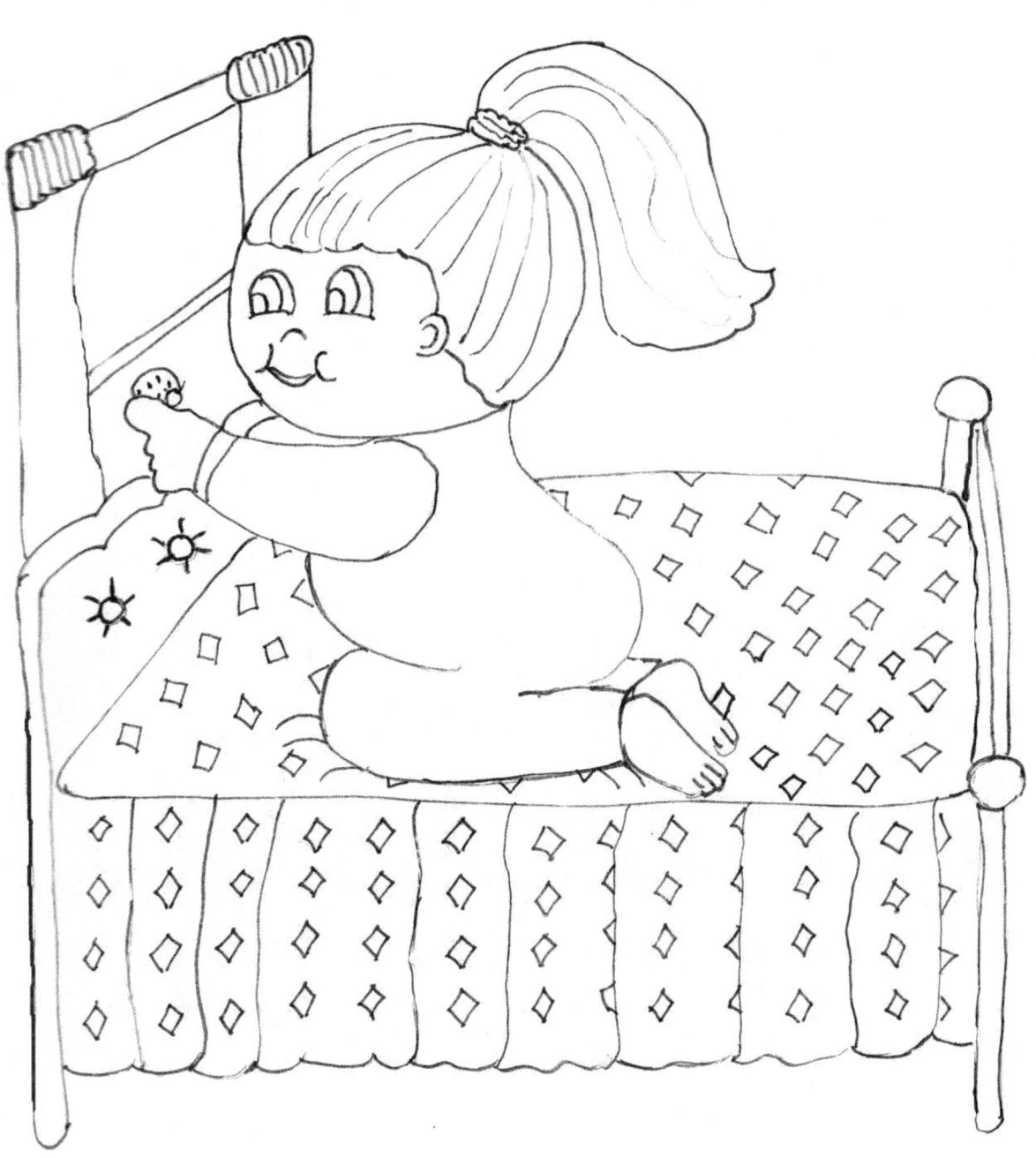

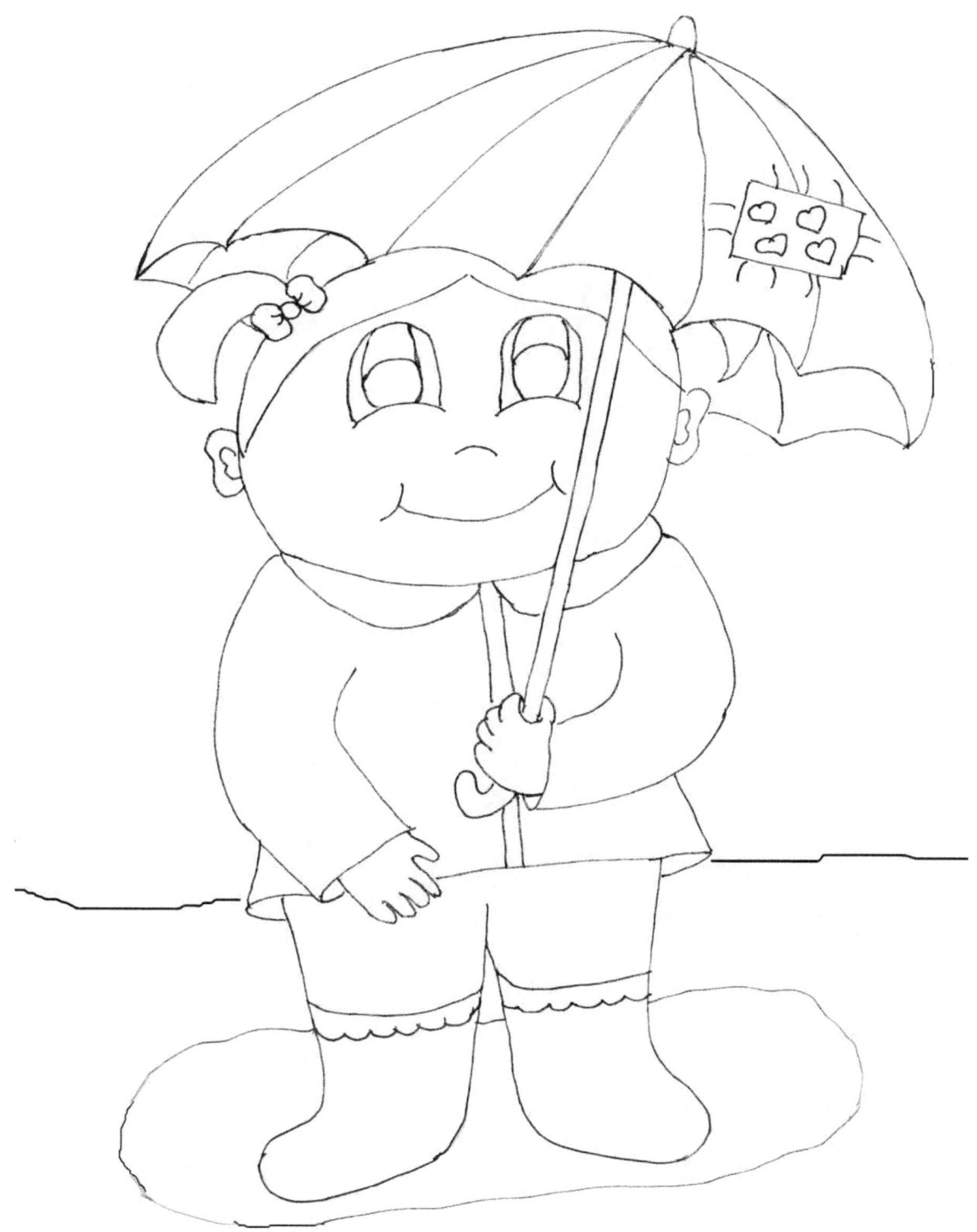

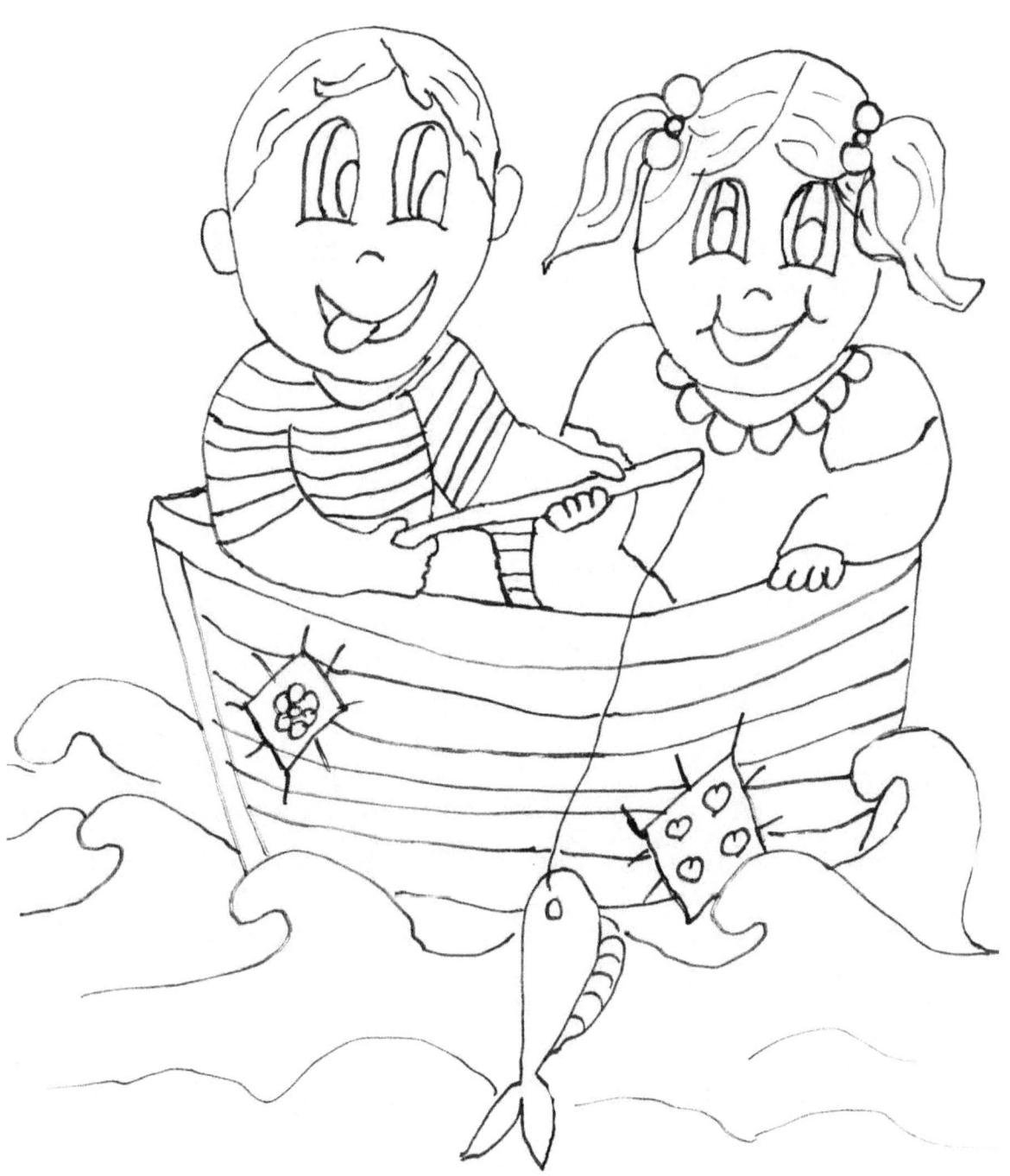

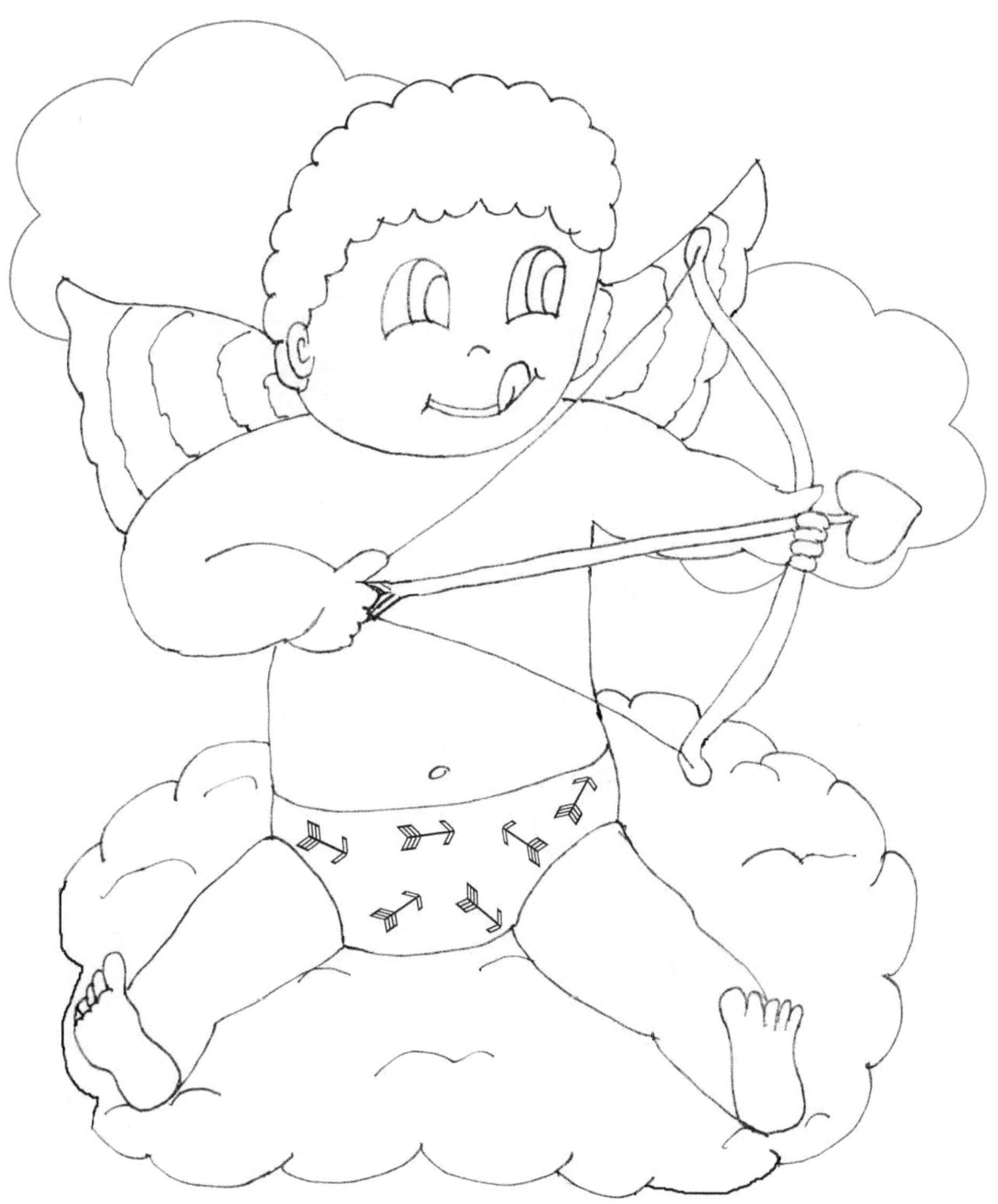

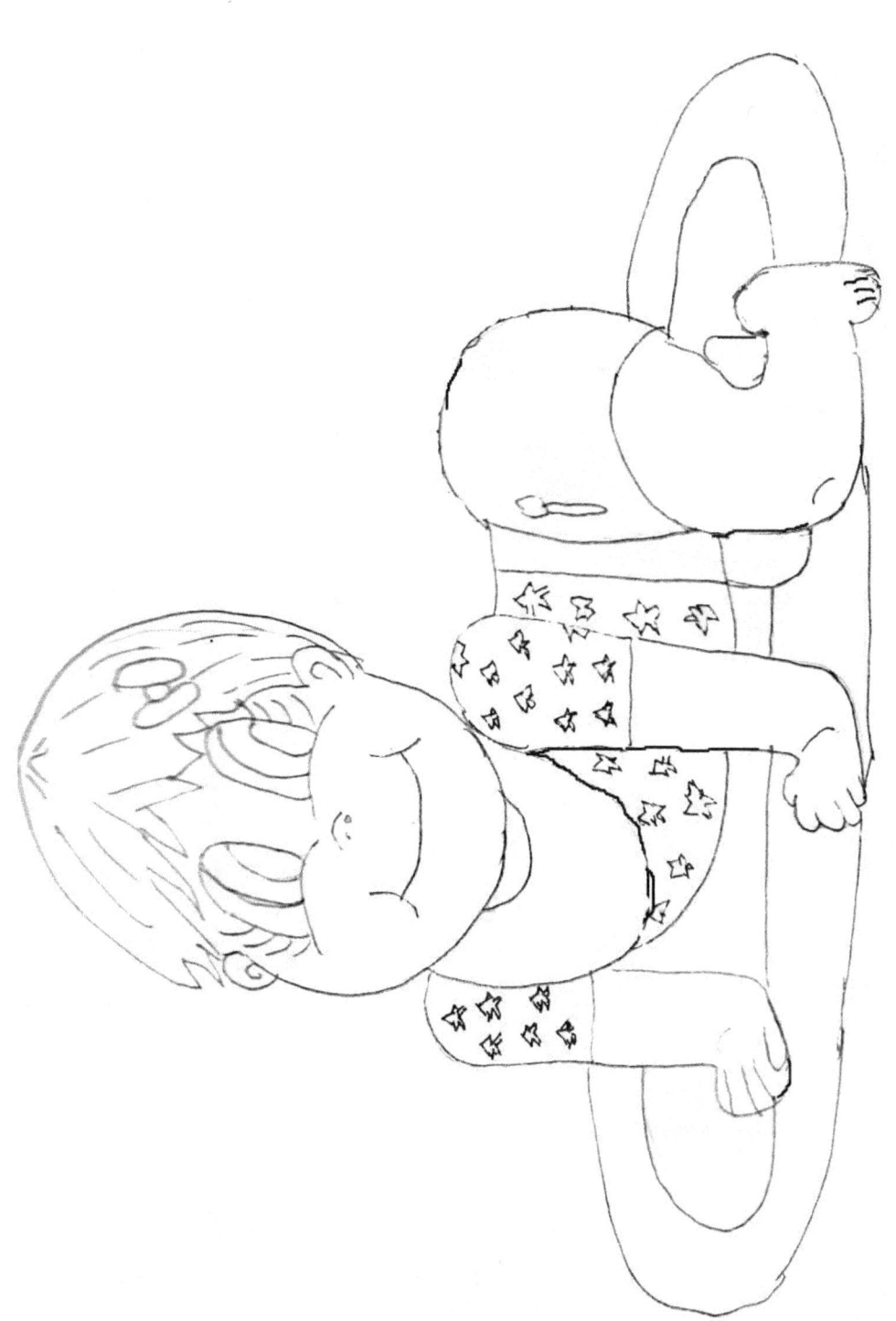

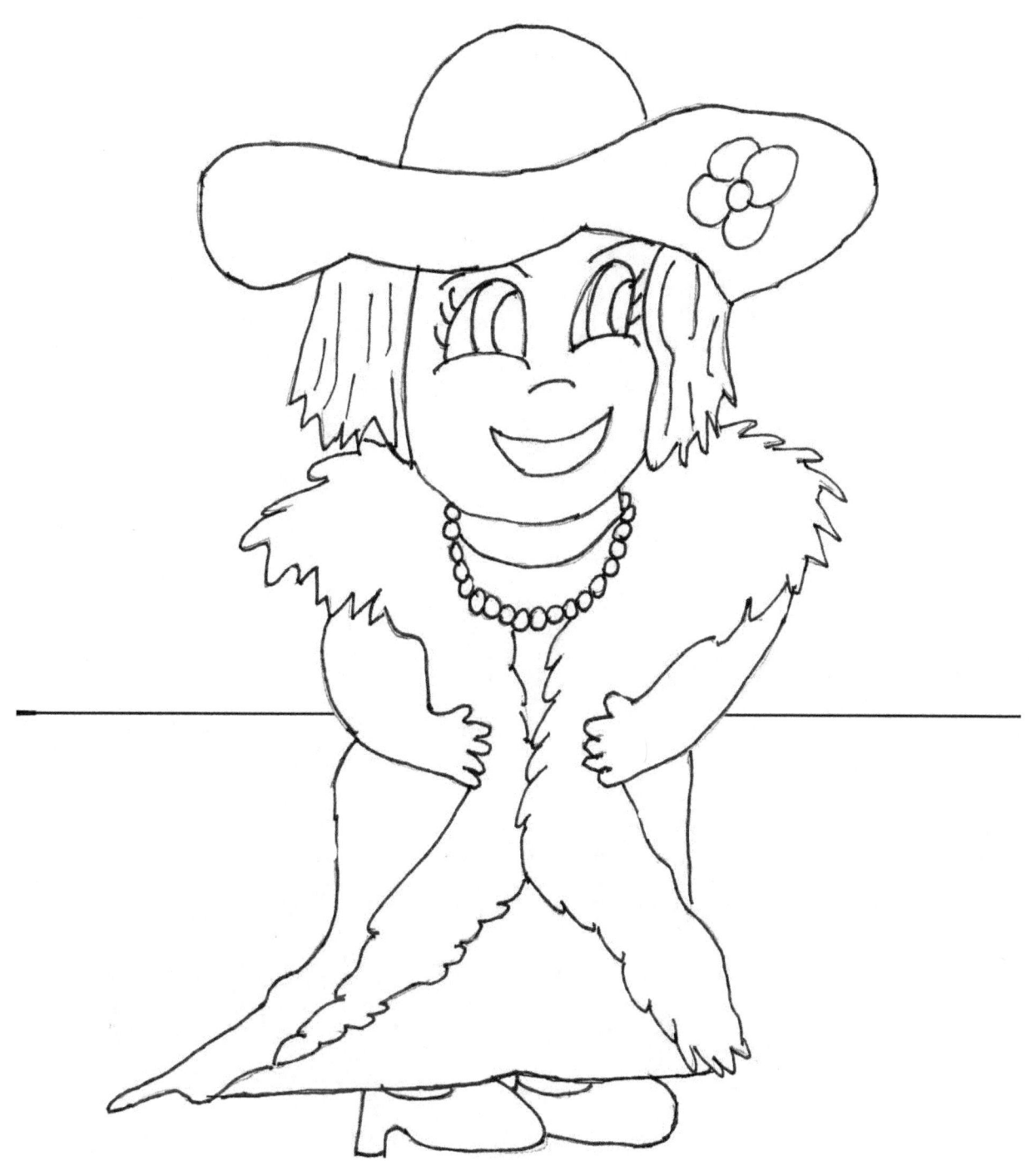

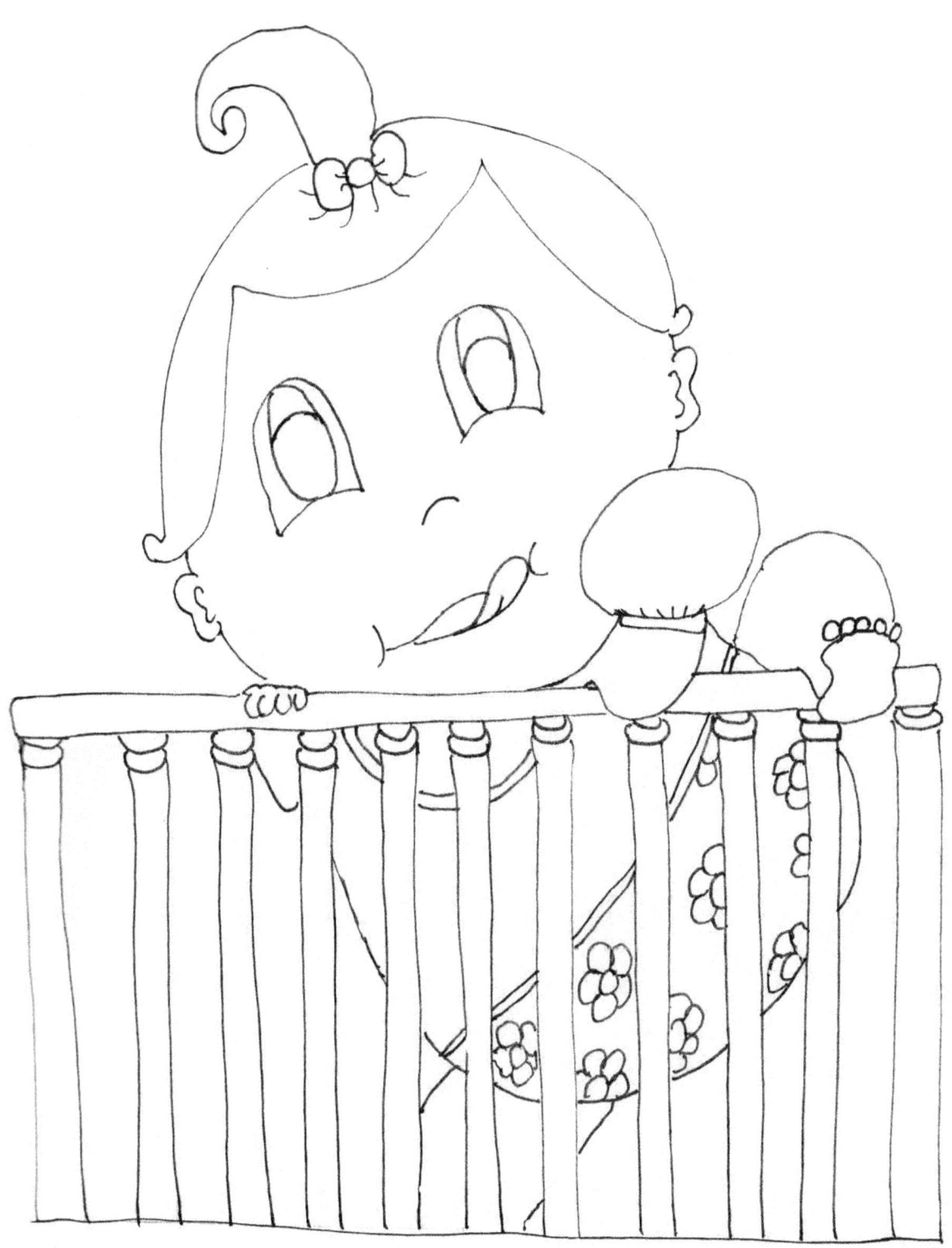

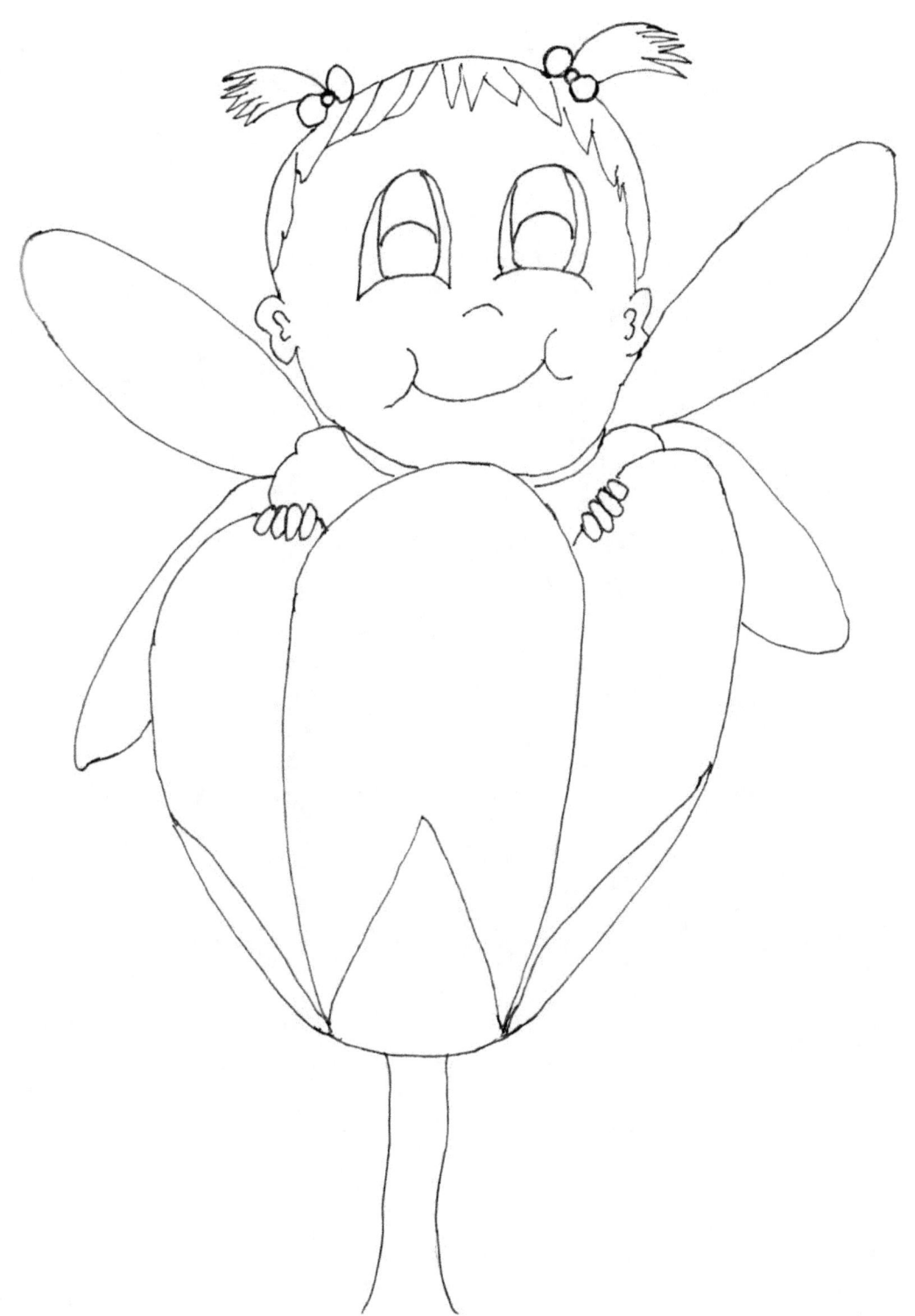

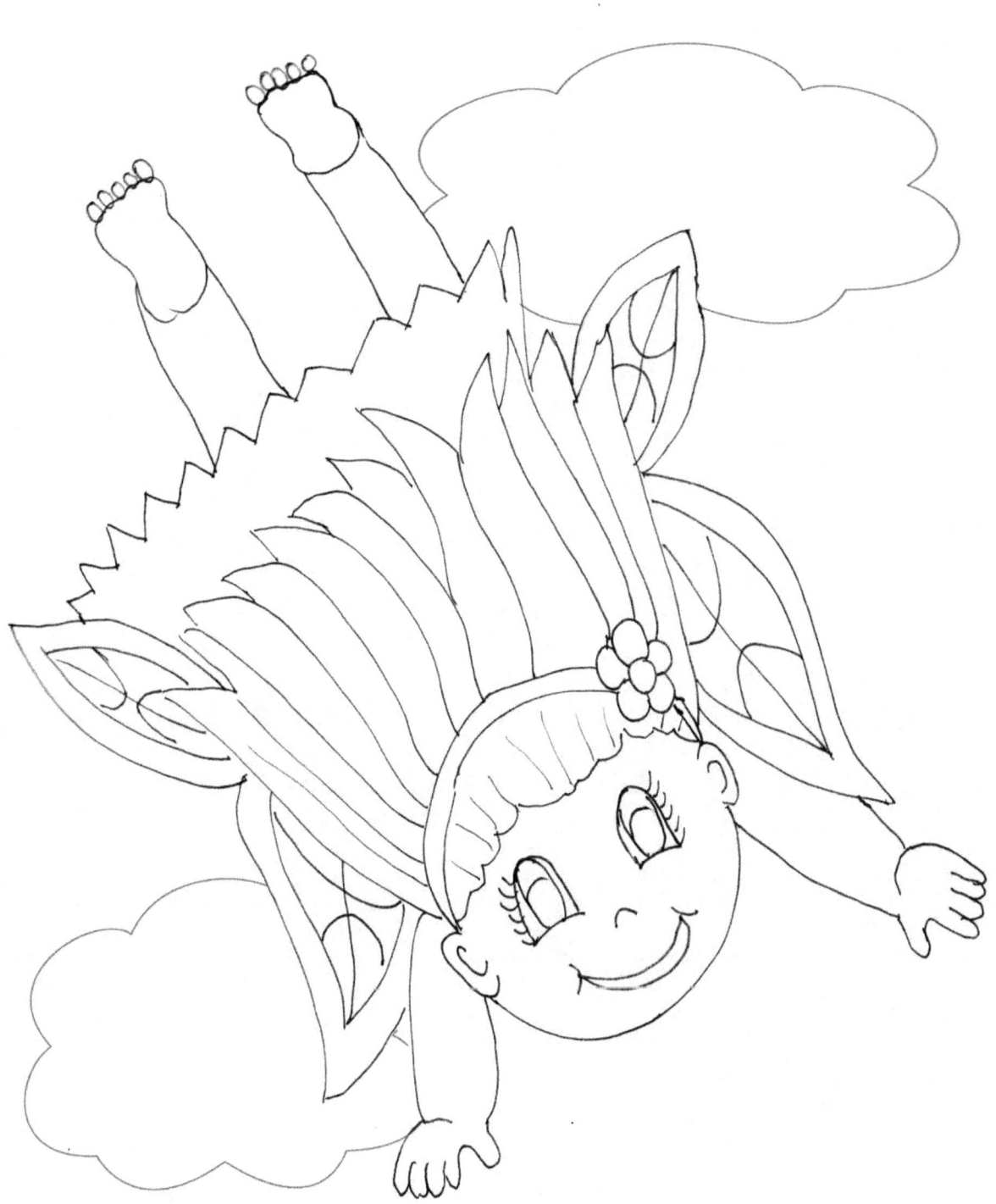

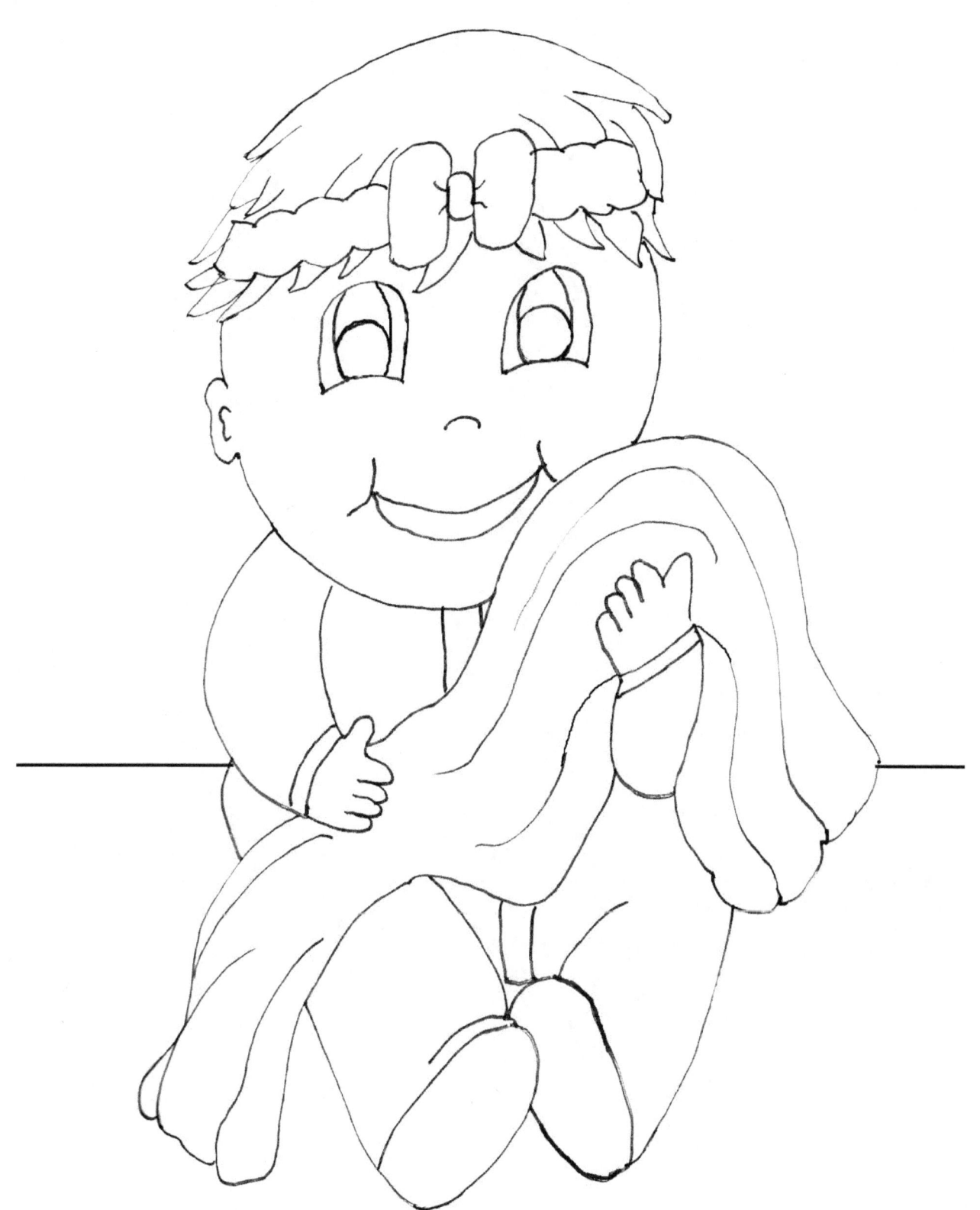

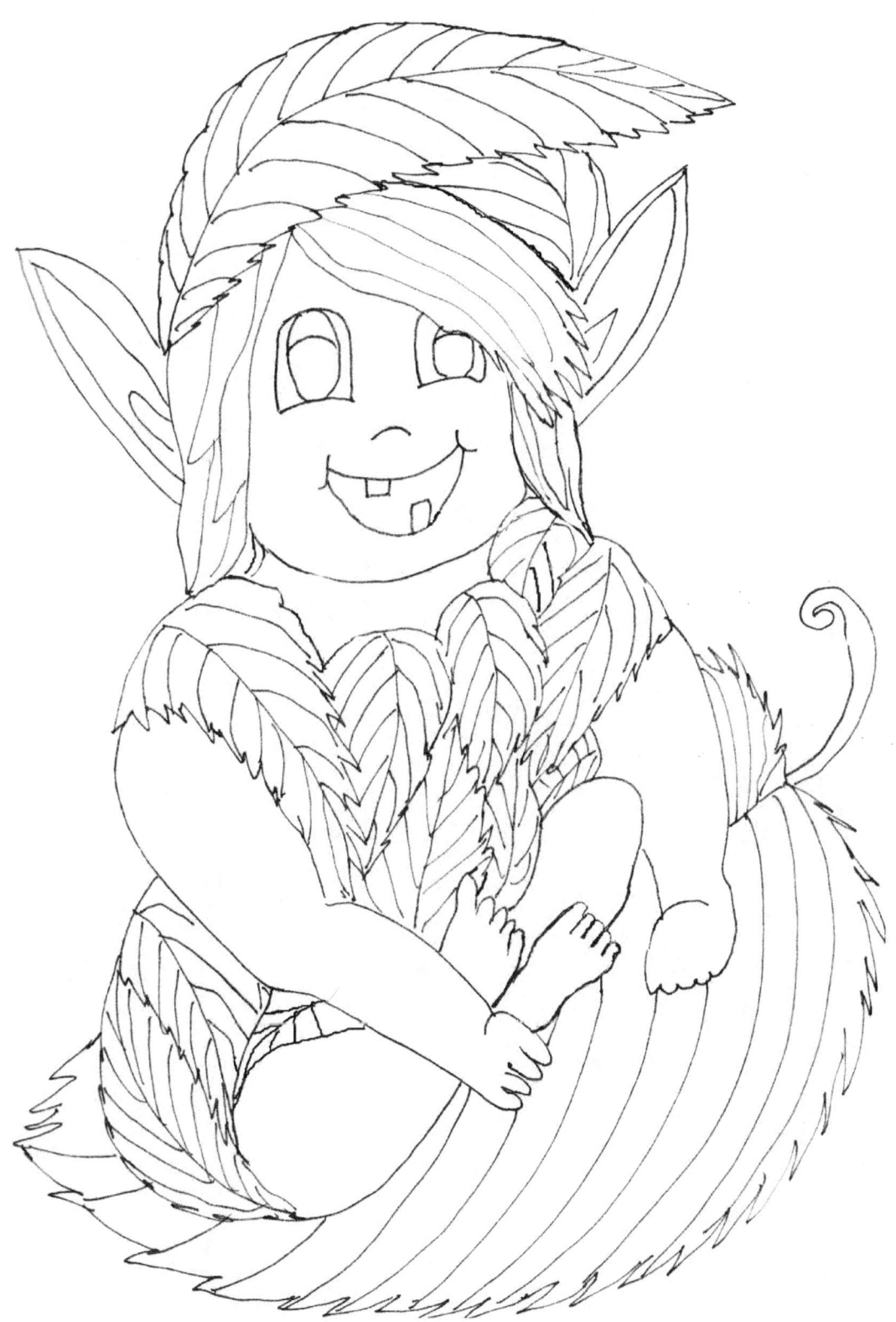

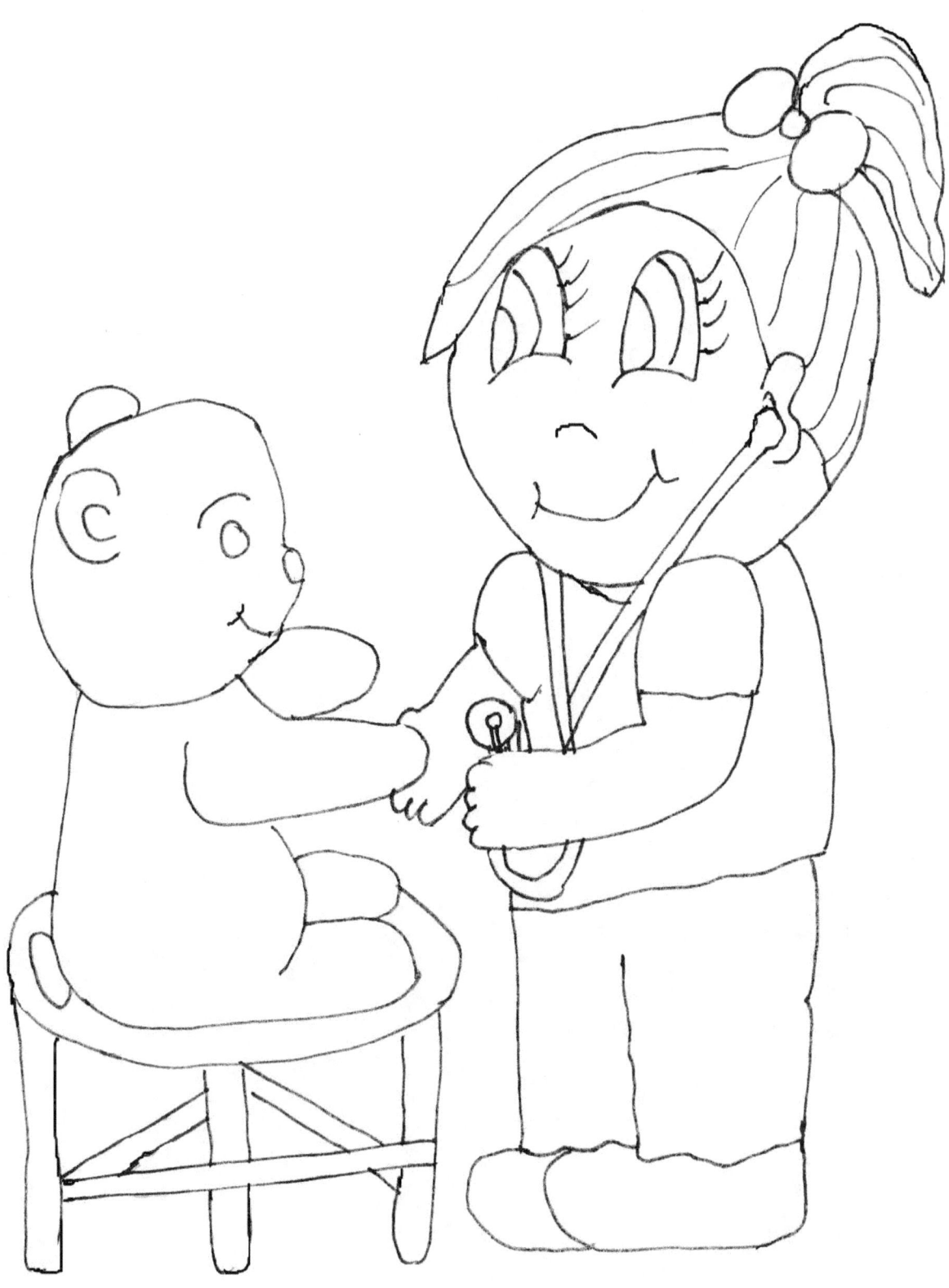

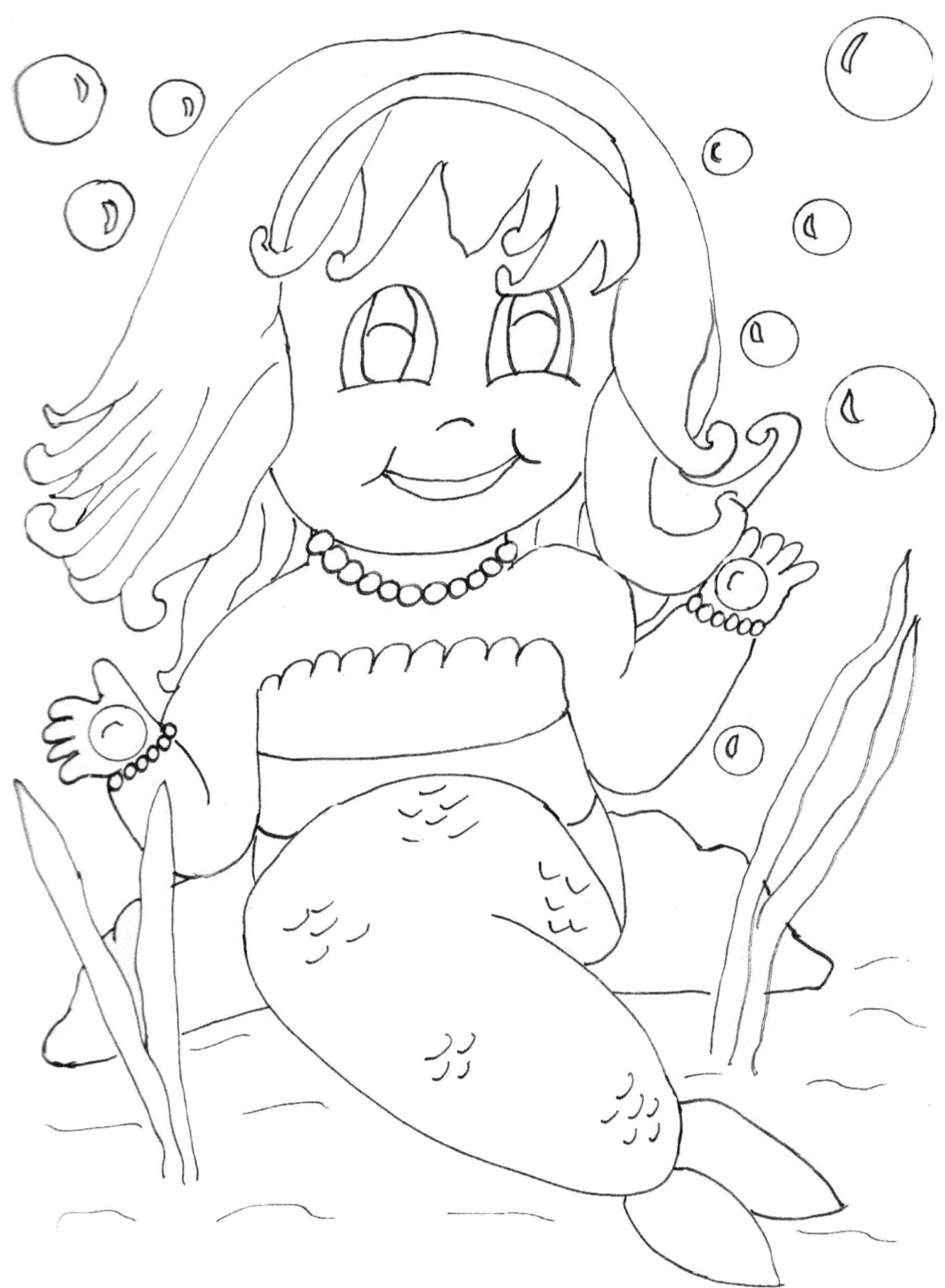

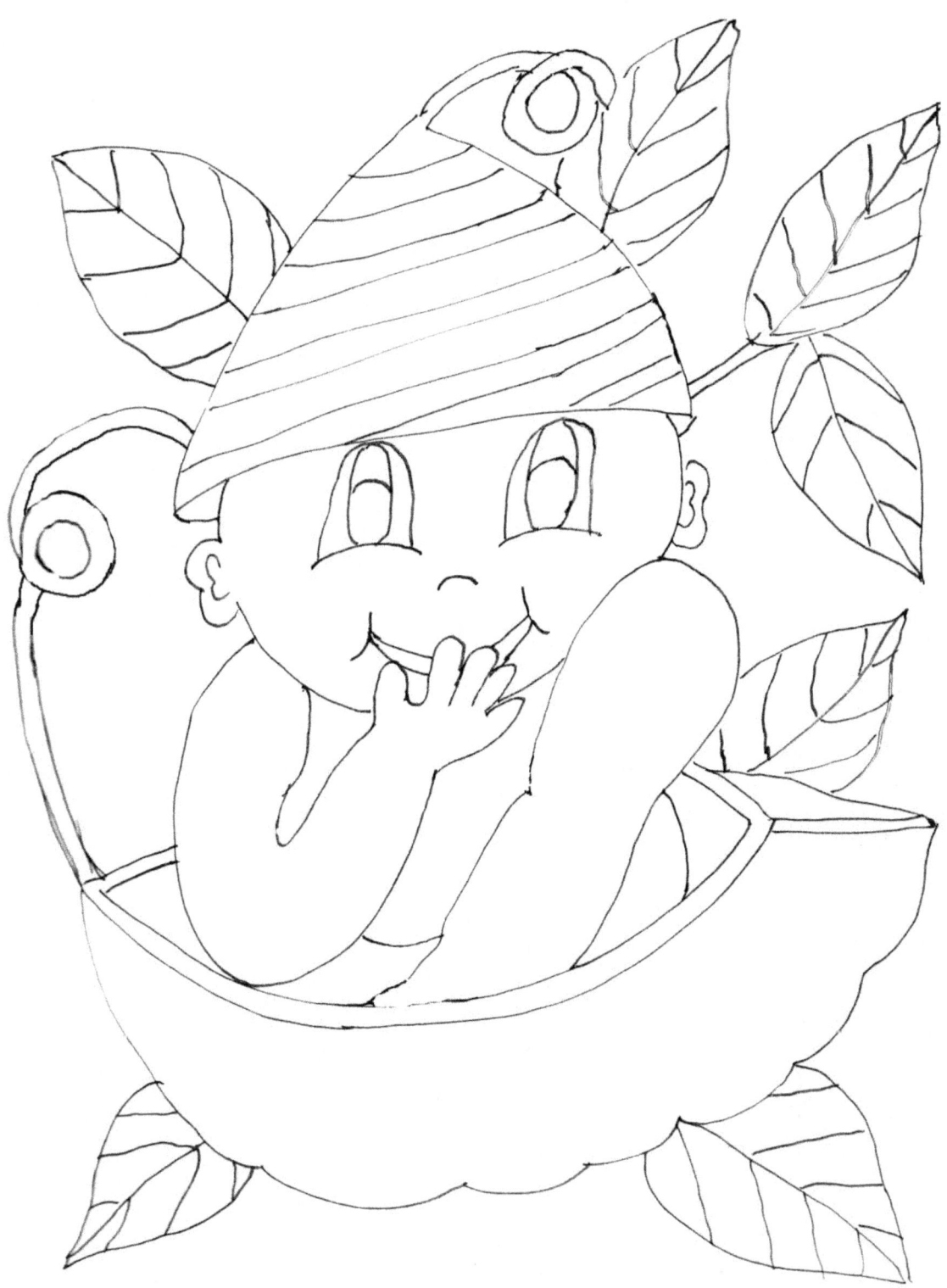

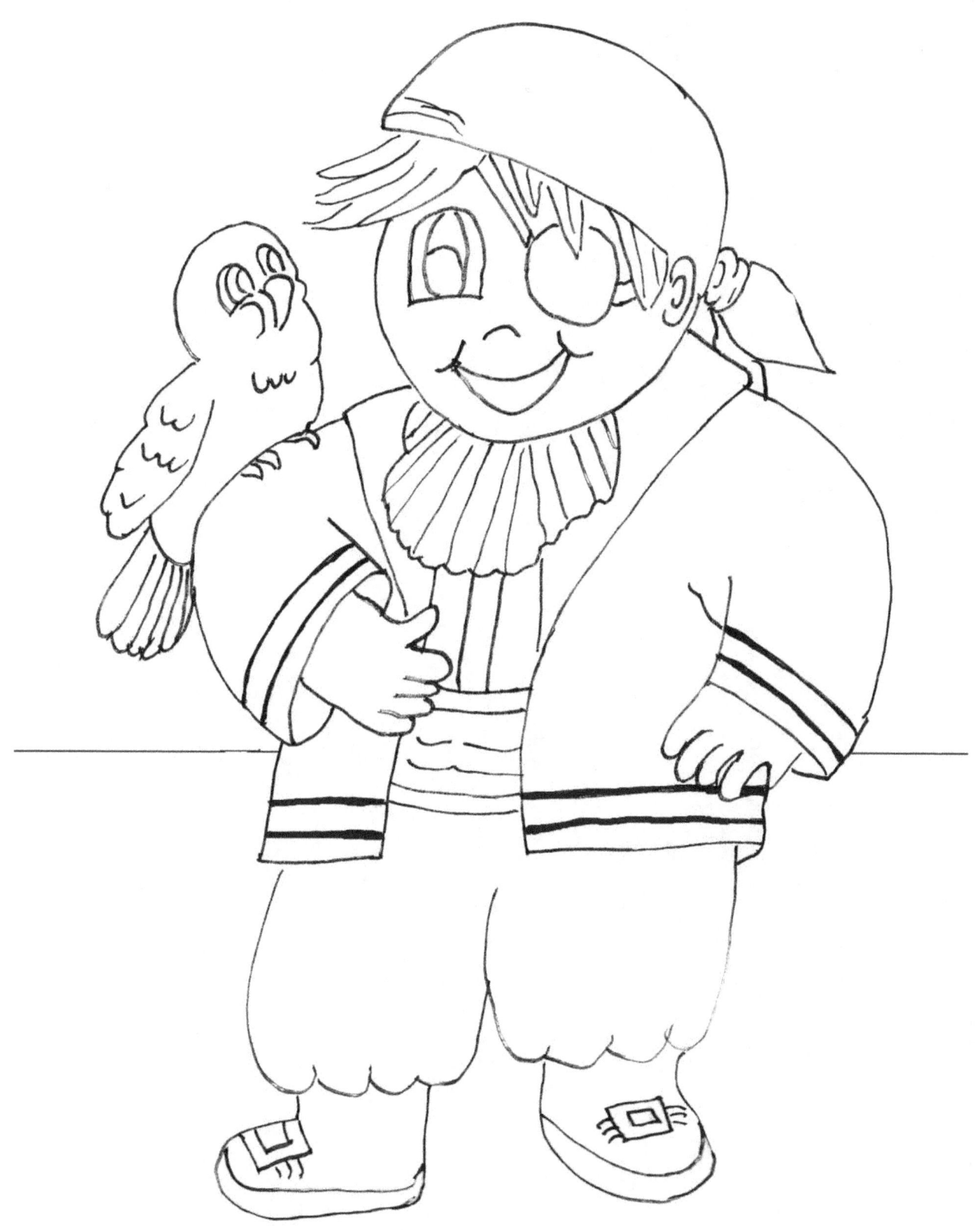

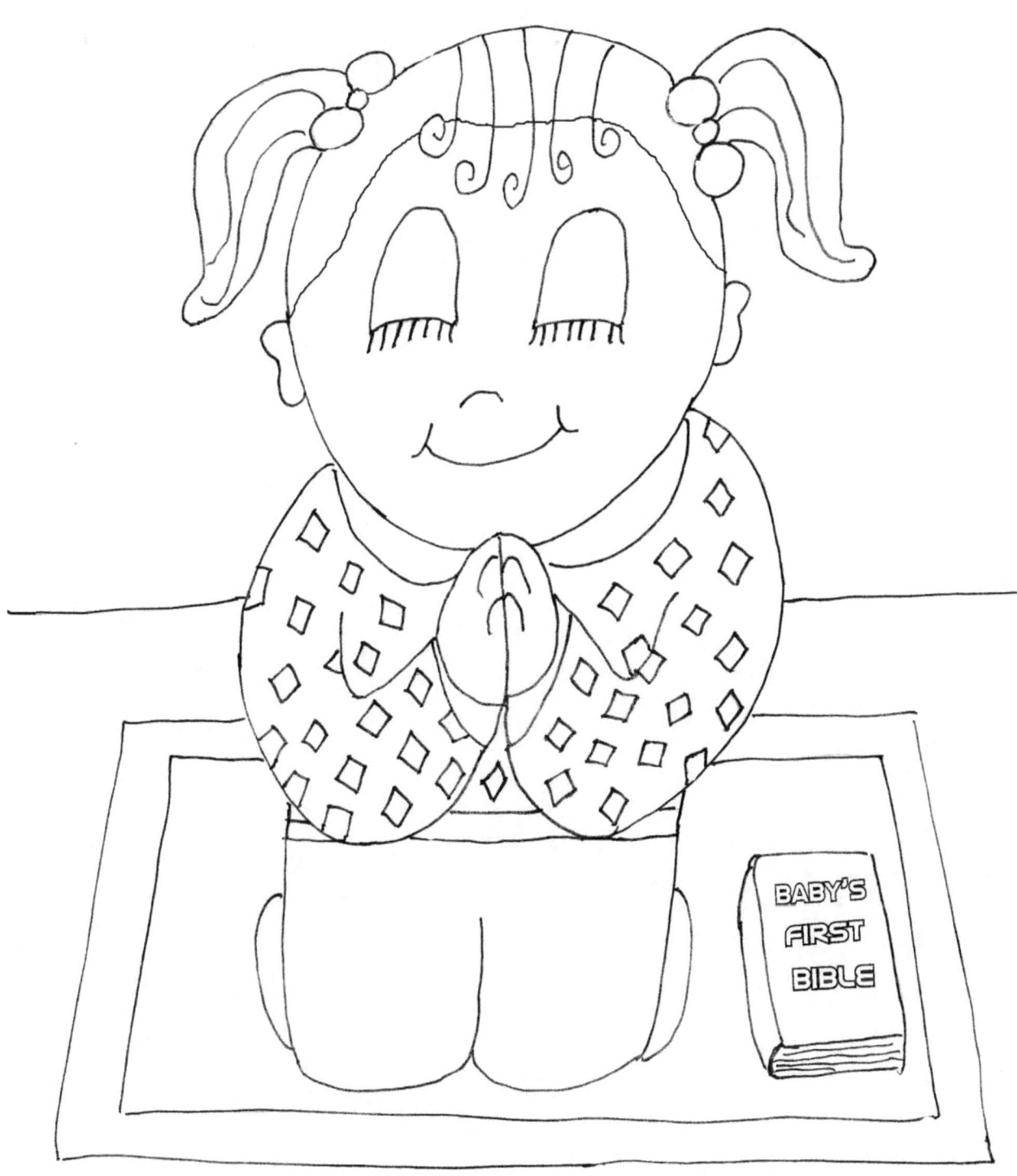

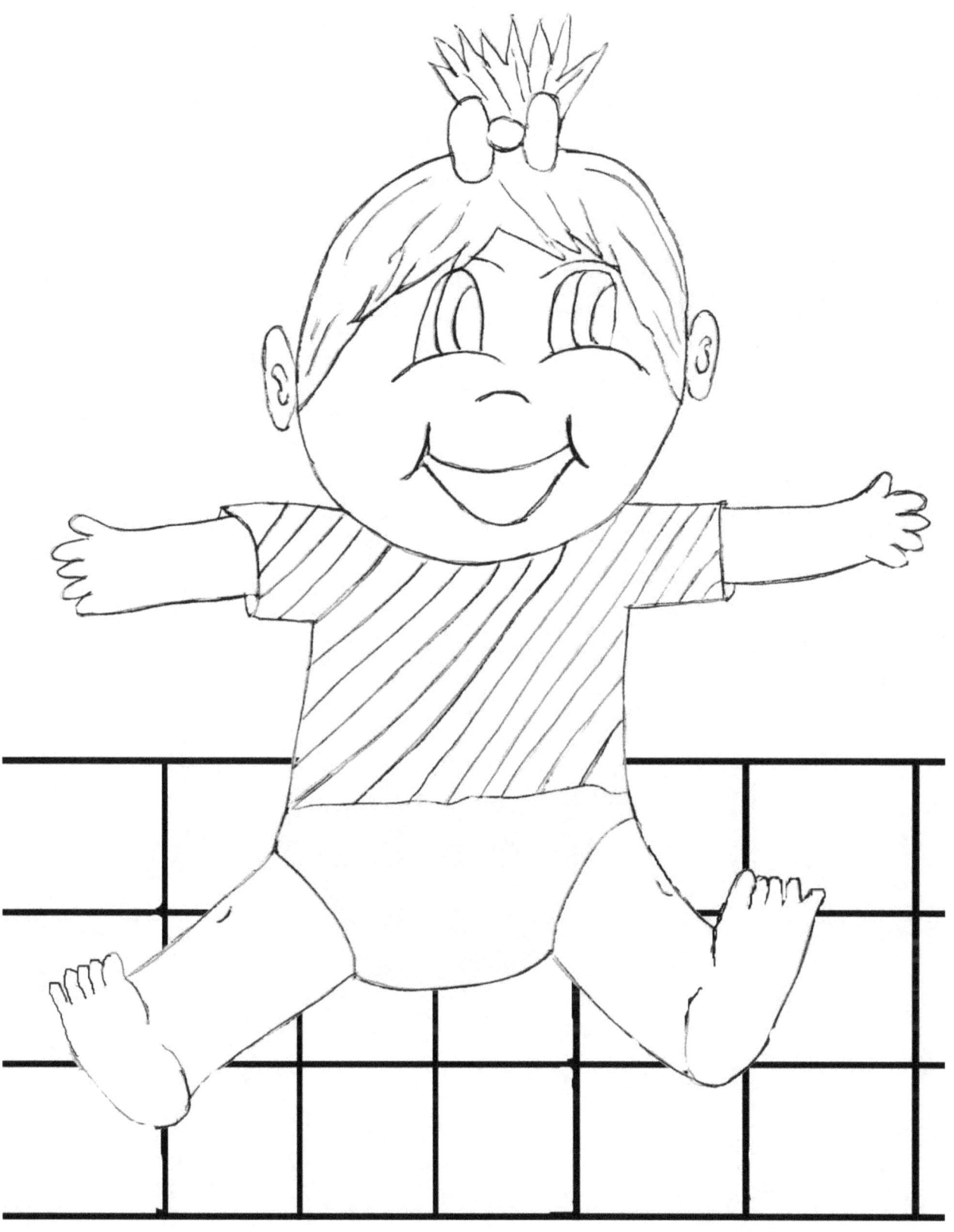

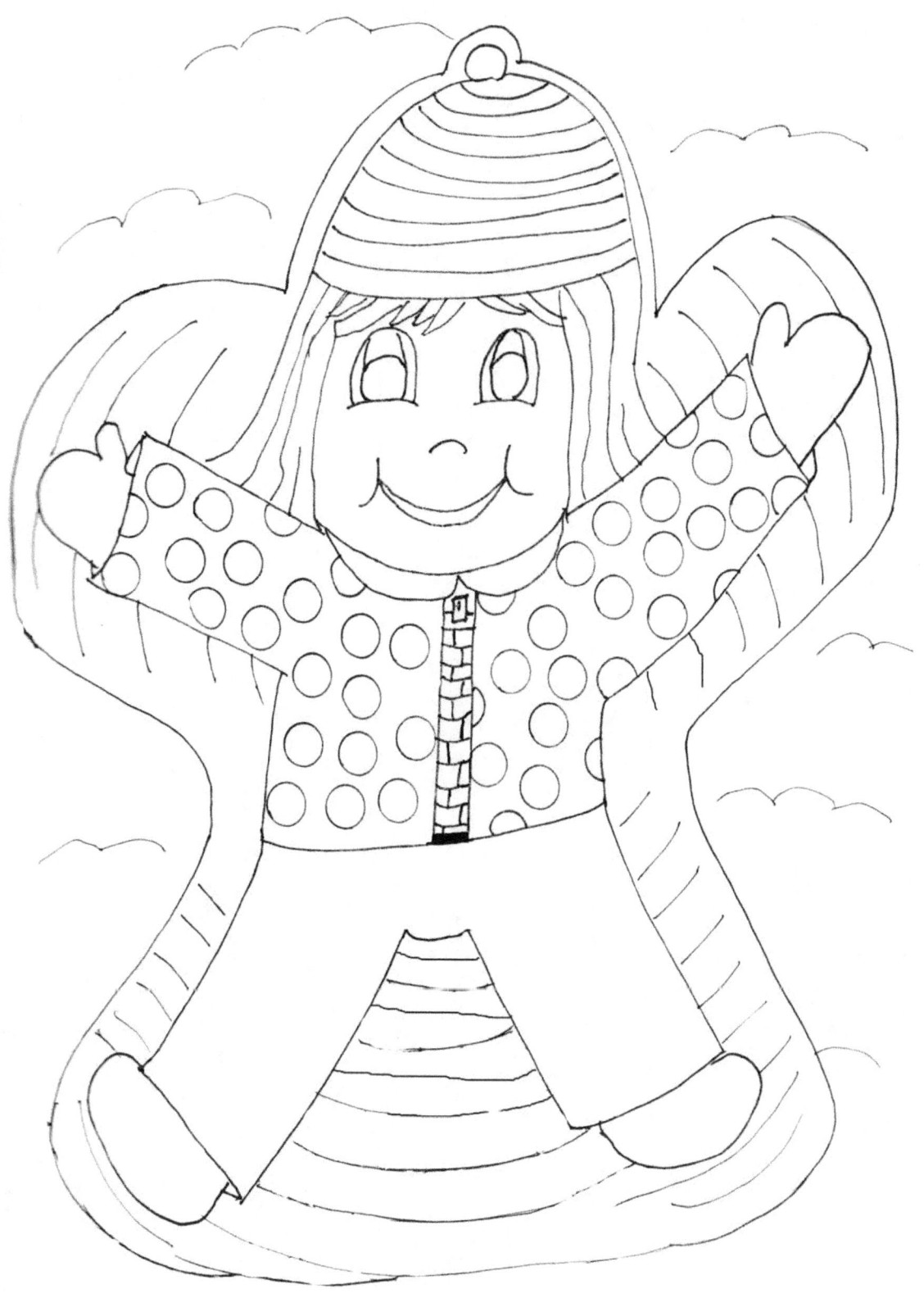

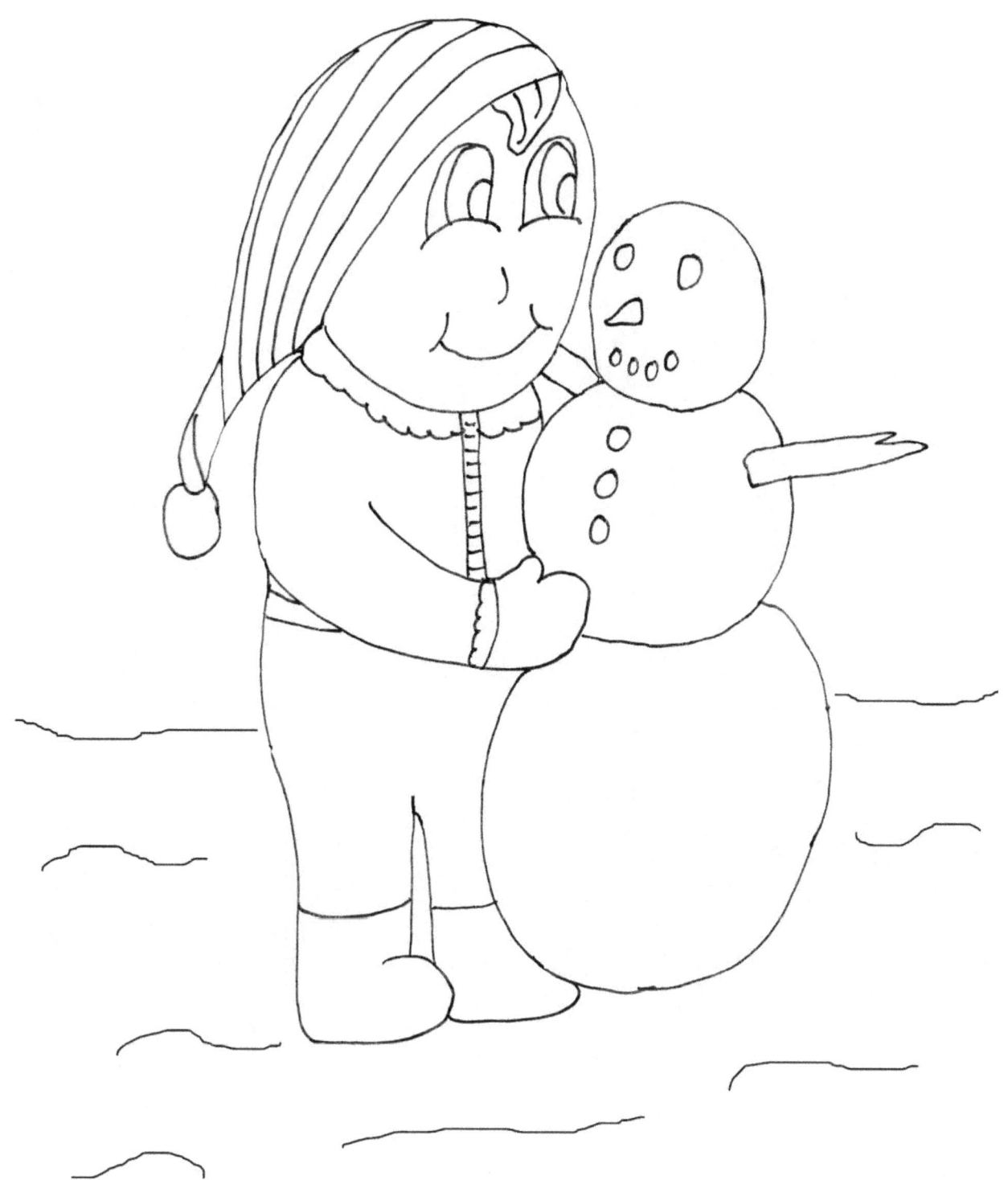

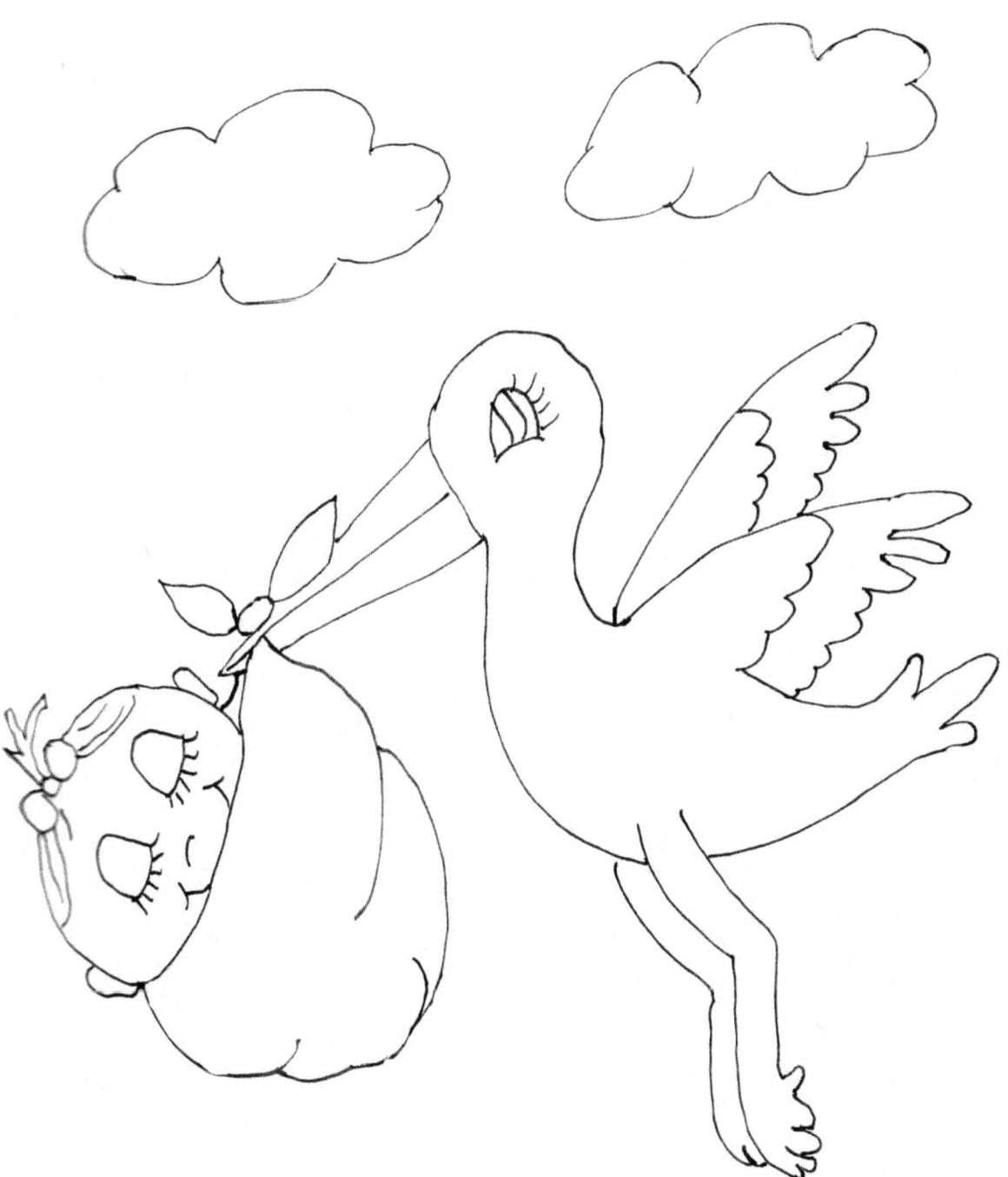

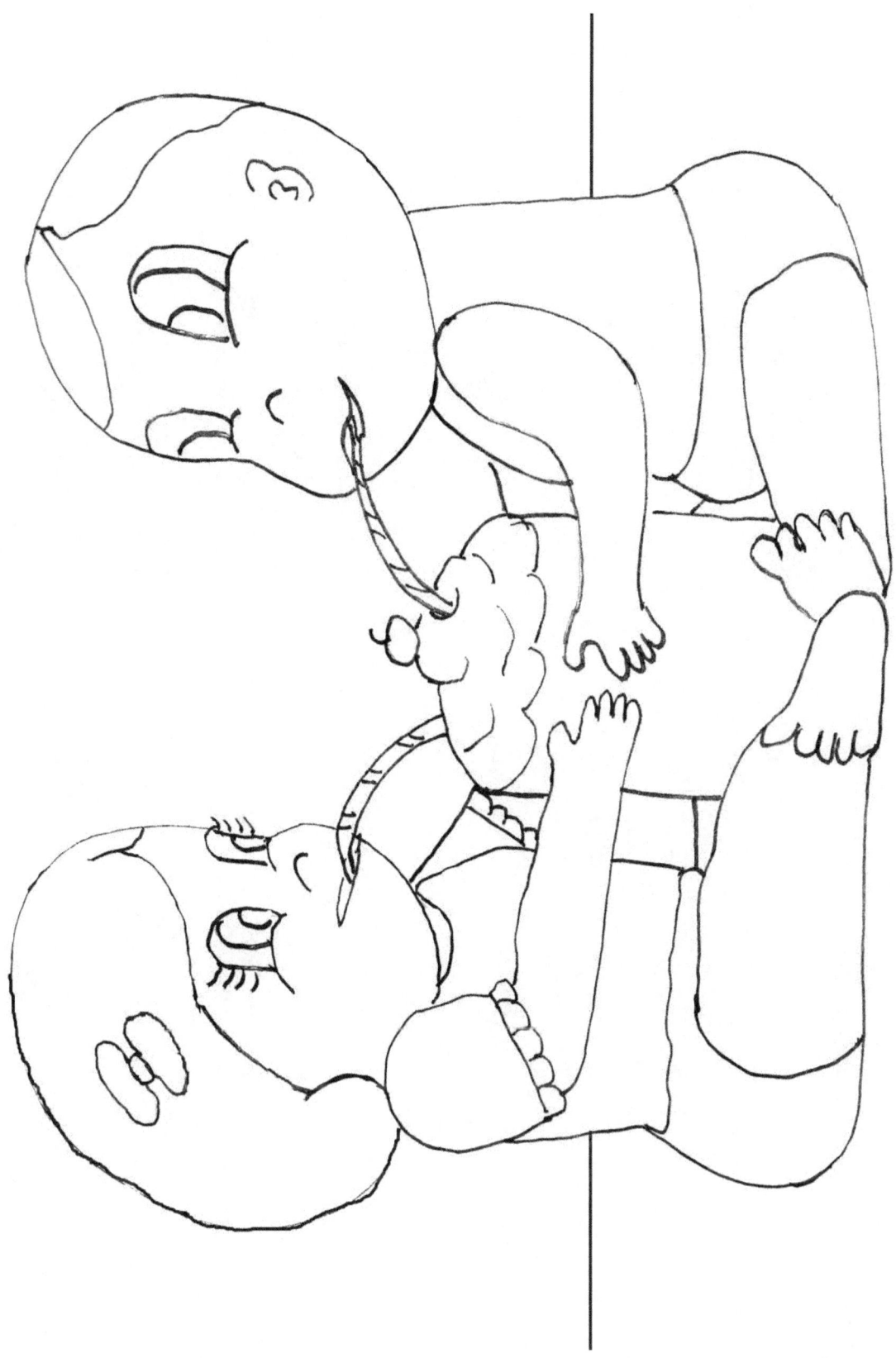

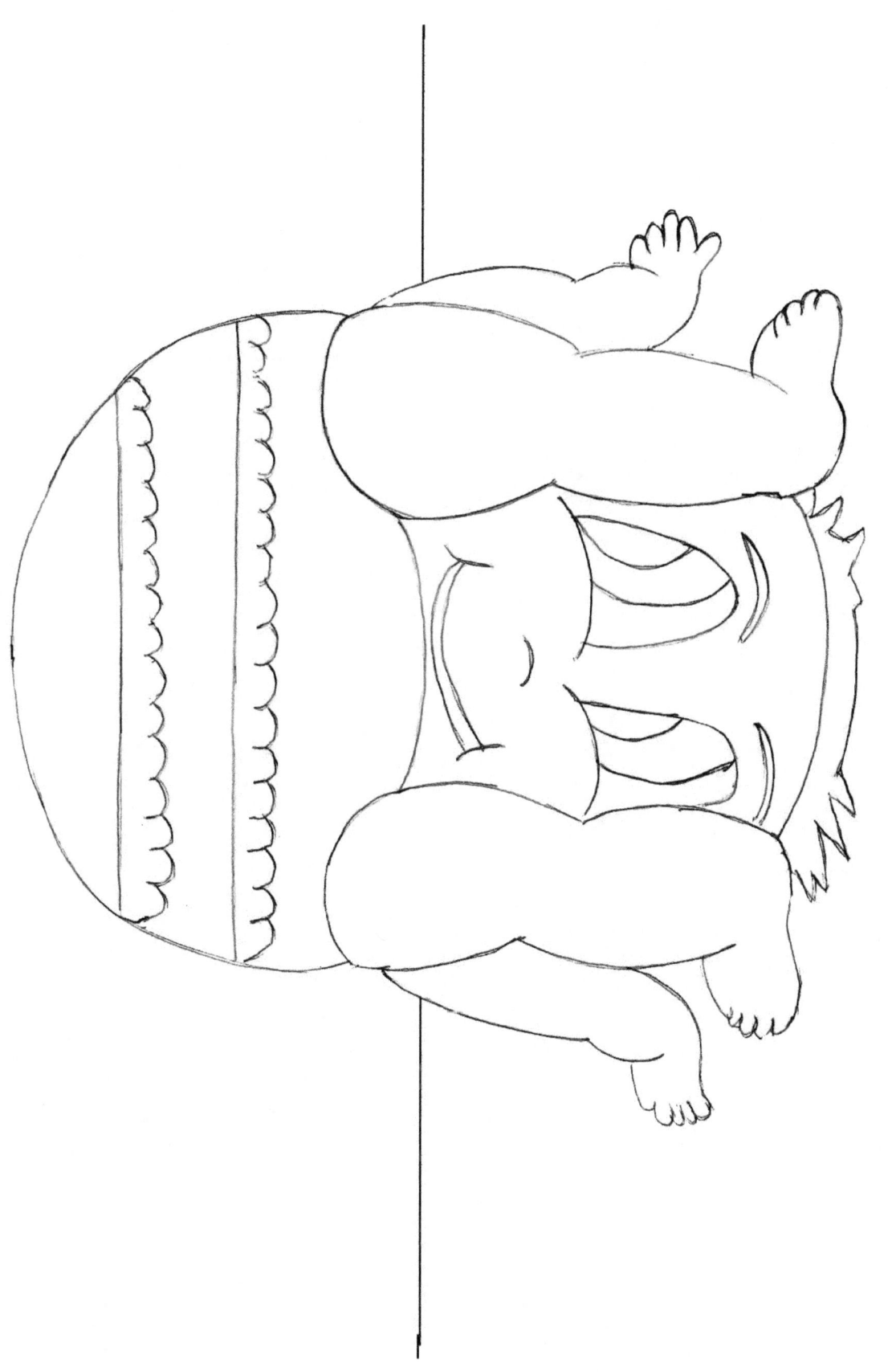

www.ingramcontent.com/pod-product-compliance
Lightning Source LLC
Chambersburg PA
CBHW080715190526
45169CB00006B/2386